ADV[illegible]

"This is the book tha[illegible]
won't just round up the usual travel suspects, information you can find anywhere. It will ferret out the places
locals love, the pubs and inns and jaw-dropping sights
that you might blow right past if you didn't know better. Which you now will, because you'll buy this book."

— **Leslie Dixon**, screenwriter, *Mrs. Doubtfire, Thomas Crown Affair, Limitless*

"Zeneba Bowers and Matt Walker capture the energy, wit, and charm of small-town Ireland by delivering great step-by-step travel suggestions in their own energetic, witty, and charming style. Reading their work will transport you, inspire you, and, most importantly, empower you to discover the small miracles that are to be found in Ireland's small towns."

— **Robert Firpo-Cappiello**, Editor-in Chief, *Budget Travel Magazine*

"Ireland is the land of céad míle fáilte—a hundred thousand welcomes. We love to welcome visitors with a wee taste of Irish warmth and hospitality. So when visitors really want to get to know us, to get off the beaten tourist track, to get under our skin (or beneath the bog!) we are only to happy to help. If you follow this wonderful guide by Zeneba Bowers and Matt Walker, lovingly researched and beautifully written, I have no doubt you will enjoy an unforgettable and authentic experience of the Emerald Isle."

— **Tony Macaulay**, author, *Paperboy*

Ireland

Small-town Itineraries for the Foodie Traveler

Zeneba Bowers
Matt Walker

Note: Since this is a "Kindle MatchBook" you can download the Amazon Kindle for free, along with any updates, delivered automatically.

Ireland

Small-town Itineraries for the Foodie Traveler

Zeneba Bowers & Matt Walker

F I R S T   E D I T I O N

ISBN: 978-1-942545-93-4
Library of Congress Control Number: 2017910409

All photography by Zeneba Bowers and Matt Walker.
Maps by Laura Atkinson. Book design by Nancy Cleary.

Little Roads Publishing
An Imprint of Wyatt-MacKenzie

www.LittleRoadsEurope.com

Table of Contents

Map of Ireland v
Our Goals vi
About this Book vii
Introduction xix

ROUTE #1 1

Southwestern Ireland

ROUTE #2 44

Western Ireland
County Clare and Vicinity

ROUTE #3 72

Western Ireland

Counties Galway, Mayo, Sligo

ROUTE #4 106

Northwest Ireland

ROUTE #5 136

Northern Ireland

ROUTE #6 178

Eastern Ireland (around Dublin)

ROUTE #7 204

Southeastern Ireland

ROUTE #8 242

Central Ireland

Appendix 263

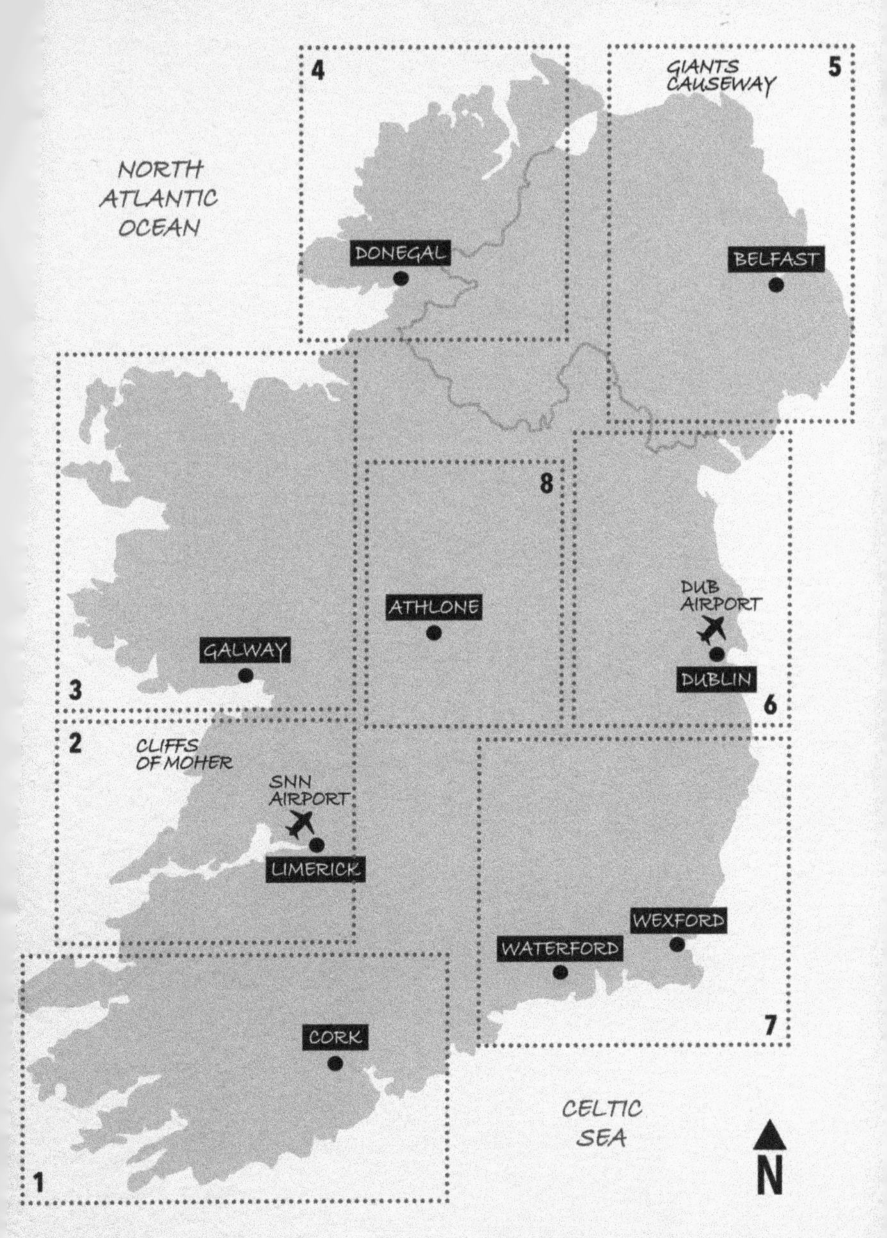
4
GIANTS CAUSEWAY
5
NORTH ATLANTIC OCEAN
DONEGAL
BELFAST
8
ATHLONE
DUB AIRPORT
DUBLIN
GALWAY
3
6
2
CLIFFS OF MOHER
SNN AIRPORT
LIMERICK
WEXFORD
WATERFORD
CORK
7
CELTIC SEA
N
1

OUR GOALS

Wherever we travel, our goals are always the same:

★ Adapting to the culture and interacting with the locals;

★ Experiencing life beyond what one finds as a typical tourist;

★ Slowing down and allowing ourselves time to take in everything around us;

★ Learning about the food, culture and history of the area; and

★ Avoiding tourist crowds whenever possible.

ABOUT THIS BOOK

This guide is for travelers who want to get away from the tourist-heavy routes—to explore out-of-the-way villages and winding back roads, to seek out authentic, memorable experiences. To immerse themselves into Ireland—its people, its places, its culture, and its food.

Rather than presenting a set of strict, day-by-day itineraries, we have created each itinerary of this book to be loose, guided by your own pace and your own tastes. We would advise spending as much as a week for each one, and more time if you have it. Our philosophy of travel hinges on taking the time to absorb the surroundings and experience a place fully, rather than running from one thing to the next in order to complete a checklist.

In this book we present an overview of our favorite sights, restaurants, lodgings, and things to do in each area that we've experienced first-hand. It's a sampling of Ireland, not a comprehensive guide. We don't cover every region of Ireland, and within each itinerary there are countless places of interest that we don't cover. Those wanting information about the Blarney Stone, the Ring of Kerry, the Book of Kells, the Rock of Cashel, or other tourist hot-spots or major cities can find it in many other guidebooks.

This guide is for those looking for something more, something different, something real—and without lots of crowds. While we do touch briefly upon a few such sights—e.g., the Cliffs of Moher, the Giant's Causeway—we do so with an effort to experience them with crowds at a minimum (or even at zero!).

Each itinerary begins with a map showing most of the places we're visiting. These maps are only for general orientation and planning purposes—you'll need to have a good map to actually navigate to and from the various locations. There are several smart-phone apps with GPS functionality that are good for this, but for us there's no substitute for an up-to-date folding map, despite the challenge of re-folding the thing. (And some of us "old-timers" still like to circle our points of interest with one of those pencil things.)

Planning a Trip to Ireland

When planning a trip to Ireland, the typical tendency is to cover as much ground as possible and see the most popular sights—the Bushmills distillery, the Book of Kells, the Waterford Crystal factory. We encourage you to throw out that checklist, as it is the same list as that of thousands of other tourists. An overly-packed schedule is a harsh mistress; if you wanted a minute-by-minute to-do list, you could have stayed at work. If you want an authentic experience, you need to allow yourself time to have one: Time to have a long lunch or an extra pint at the pub, to enjoy some craic with the locals, to explore a side street or an unexpected sight, to relax and breathe and take it all in.

As itinerary planners, we have talked many clients out of some of the "must-see" destinations in favor of little-known places. They always return rested, fulfilled, and carrying life-long memories of their experiences.

The excursions in this book will guide you through some of the most beautiful countryside, take you to some fascinating locations, and lead you to some of the most delicious food and drink experiences you'll ever find.

Our way of traveling is different

As professional classical musicians, Zeneba is the Artistic Director and Matt is the Operations Manager of the Grammy-nominated ALIAS Chamber Ensemble. We put a great deal of time and thought into creating interesting and diverse programs for concerts. By the time we founded the group, we had already performed much of the standard and often-heard music by famous composers. We decided to try something more adventurous. As a result the ensemble made a name for itself for commissioning new music, finding and performing great but unusual pieces by little-known composers, and occasionally offering lesser-known works by the great masters. The result became an eclectic concert experience that has something for everyone, while introducing audiences to new ways of listening to music.

When we started traveling to Europe, we applied the same general idea to our travel philosophy: After checking off the obligatory visits to the A-list locations (the Roman Colosseum, the Tower of London, Venice, Stonehenge, and the like), we started looking for more authentic, out-of-the-way experiences. We found them down the little roads of Europe—the small towns, the remote abbeys and castles, the ruins of Roman outposts, and of course the Grandma's-kitchen cuisine. This was a more immersive experience, visiting places without tourists but rich with culture, art, architecture, history, and food.

A few notes about visiting Ireland

Historic Sites

Ireland is dotted with countless historic sites from several periods, and this guide will lead you to some of our favorites. Most of these can be divided broadly into three main types, as follows:

Pre-historic Irish megaliths

Ireland's' landscape is dotted with countless megaliths, structures built in the Bronze Age (around 1000-3000 BC) or earlier from one or more huge stones. These come in a variety of forms, from stone circles, like the famous Stonehenge, to burial chambers ("*dolmens*") and forts, as well as single inscribed standing stones. The stones typically weigh many tons, and some of them were lifted and moved from hundreds of miles away. Many of these structures were built to align with distant geography or astronomical events: solstices and equinoxes, planetary motions, solar cycles. They are incredible testaments to prehistoric human ingenuity and surprising astronomical understanding, as well as to their deep sense of spirituality. In this guide we use the terms "megalithic", "prehistoric" and "Neolithic" to refer in general to such stone structures.

Early Christian sites

When Christianity was spread widely to Ireland in the 4th-5th centuries (by the fabled Saints Patrick, Brigit, and Columba, among others), many Christian settlements were founded at pilgrimage waypoints. Traces of these dating from the 6th-9th century can be found all over the country, in the form of churches, dwellings, and inscribed stones, and later, the iconic Irish high crosses and round towers. Early Christians sometimes built these sites on top of pre-Christian temples or other sacred pagan places like megalithic sites. They often became the base of more lasting religious buildings in the following medieval period.

Medieval religious sites and King Henry VIII "suppression"

The middle ages—roughly 1000-1500 AD—saw the establishment of many Christian monasteries, abbeys, priories, and friaries. Though the words were specific to the particular sects and their organization, in this guide we use the words less strictly. Visitors will find that most of these medieval settlements are in various states of ruin. We have England's King Henry VIII to thank for this: When he "suppressed" and "dissolved" (that's medieval-royalty-talk for "destroyed" and "pillaged") the monasteries in his rebellion against the Catholic church in the mid-1500s, few if any of these settlements remained afterwards. Some of them were partly restored in later centuries, but many fell into disrepair, becoming an eerie and poignant part of Irish landscape and history.

Gaelic-Irish language

Although nearly everyone that you'll meet in Ireland speak English, it's not the national language; Irish is. Sometimes called Gaelic Irish, it's connected to Scottish Gaelic, as the two nations are a mere dozen miles apart at some points along the coast. Irish is a musical tongue, spoken by nearly a fifth of the Irish population, and recent efforts are underway to revive use of the language still further. Signs are in both languages, often in Irish first, nearly everywhere. In remote areas, especially on the west coast, the signs may well be in Irish only, and you may encounter a few people who speak almost no English at all. If this happens, remember that you're in their backyard, so be polite and use a lot of pantomime to get your point across.

Just a couple of words you'll want to be familiar with:

Fáilte (FEL-cha) - "Welcome"

Cead mile failte - a thousand welcomes"
Sláinte (SLAN-cha) - "Cheers!"

Craic (Crack) - Good times eating, drinking, socializing

Go raibh maith agat (guh-ruh-MAH-agut, said quickly) - "Thank you" (literally "May you have goodness")

What's On

Taps

Nearly every pub in Ireland keeps taps of Dublin's famous Guinness Stout flowing at all times, as well as Bulmer's cider. ("Cider" in Ireland is hard cider, ranging from sweet to dry, mostly less sweet than what is typical in the U.S.) In addition, you'll often see Kilkenny's delicious Smithwicks (pronounced "Smiddicks" or, in the

north, “Smith-icks”) and usually a couple of beers such as Carlsberg and Heineken. In and near County Cork, you’ll find the fine Murphy’s stout in addition to (or sometimes instead of) Guinness. Beamish stout is a less common but also delicious alternative in the southwest. In Northern Ireland you’ll see more Bass Ale—a British product. All this being said, be sure to ask about local craft brews—recent years have seen a resurgence in this art, and many excellent ales and porters yearn to stand out amongst the standard taps.

Food

Many but not all pubs offer food, and some close up their kitchens altogether in the late fall and winter. If you don’t see a sign for food, it’s good to ask if they do food as soon as you walk into a place, and if the kitchen is still on. This is all the more reason to plan ahead and reserve meals in advance, or rent a self-catering lodging. (One town we visited had an unusual arrangement: All the old local pubs—the dark, woody bars with the fireplace and the usual array of classic taps—offered no food other than bags of crisps; conversely, all the eateries were more like sit-down restaurants, offering decent food but without the *craic* of a neighborhood pub.)

Irish breakfast

The price at most B&Bs and hotels will include a breakfast in their price. These range from simple spreads (cereals, breads/pastries, yogurt, fruit) to cooked breakfasts made to order. The typical Irish breakfast—just ask for the "full Irish"—will include one or two eggs (poached or sunny-side-up unless you request otherwise), bacon *and* sausage, fried potatoes in some form, a grilled tomato, and often also baked beans and sautéed mushrooms, as well as toast and Irish brown bread. In southern Ireland you'll also get two little fried rounds of white and black pudding—that's yet more meat, not something sweet. It's sometimes a challenge to start the day with a full Irish, especially if you had a large meal the night before; but it's a delicious challenge.

Republic of Ireland / Northern Ireland

While both countries coexist perfectly peacefully on this beautiful island (and we cover both in this guide), it's important to know the distinction between Ireland and Northern Ireland. Ireland is properly called the Republic of Ireland, being its own sovereign country. Its independence from the United Kingdom came in 1922 after a six-year struggle (and after several movements in previous decades). Northern Ireland consists of those counties that remained within the authority of the Crown, and stand as one of the countries along with England, Scotland, and Wales to comprise the United Kingdom. (Historically, Ireland is Catholic, Northern Ireland is Protestant, along with the U.K.—though there is plenty of mixing in both directions, and in fact recent years has seen a growth in people who claim "none" as their religion.) Ireland uses the euro (€) and the metric system; Northern Ireland uses the British pound (£) and "standard" measurements. Luckily for those of us who love the whole island, the concept of "a pint" is universally understood and revered.

[Note: As of this writing, the border between Northern Ireland and the Republic of Ireland is open and free on all roads, large and small. However, it remains to be seen how travel here will be affected by the "Brexit" vote of 2016, in which the U.K. declared its wish to split from the European Union (of which Ireland is a member). It's also worth noting that Northern Ireland voted narrowly (about 55%-45%) to remain in the EU.]

INTRODUCTION

Ireland

For our fifth or sixth trip to the "Emerald Isle" a few years back, we had booked a stay in the Galley Head Lighthouse, down in County Cork at the very southern edge of Ireland. In communicating with the caretaker of the place, we learned that her brother-in-law is Gerald Butler, a third-generation lightkeeper. Gerald still came around regularly to check on and maintain the workings of the lighthouse. We arranged to meet him, to buy his book, and to get an impromptu tour of the lighthouse itself.

Gerald's memoir, "The Lightkeeper", tells the fascinating story of his childhood and upbringing at several lighthouses around Ireland. In one anecdote, he tells the story of an unpleasant "neighbor" when his father was stationed at the remote Ballycotton Island light. This lighthouse sits on a tiny island off the coast of east Cork, where they shared the small bit of ground there with a very aggressive billy-goat. The goat would head-butt Gerald at every opportunity; safe passage past the stubborn animal required a toll, or else. And what was the goat's currency of choice? Why, a lit cigarette, of course, which the goat would carry off and smoke in solitude.

So we were eager to meet this colorful character at the lighthouse; but first we needed to stop for lunch, and then gather provisions for our stay. We sat for a meal at a local seafood restaurant specializing in lobster, the kind of place where the server escorts you to the tank to pick out your particular decapod. We did this, expressing our slight discomfort with the idea that the fate of these crustaceans was in our hands. The server laughed: "It's a lot better now that we don't name them. We used to say, "Uh-oh, there goes Harry!'" Nevertheless, 20 minutes later, the delicious Irish butter made us forget old what's-his-name.

Now on to our food shopping. Lucky for us, it was market day in one of the towns on the way to Galley Head. Most Irish towns, large and small, have a weekly market where the local food producers sell their goods. In the center of the town, dozens of vendors gathered, each in their own little tent-stall: Fish, meat, cheese, milk, jams, breads, fruit, vegetables, various prepared foods.

We soon had enough food to last the two of us well past our stay—much of it organic, and all of it local. We resolved to consume it all.

We came across an apple farmer selling his hard cider—or rather, not selling it. He stood next to a giant crate of apples, as well as his stock of bottles. We wanted some apple juice and two ciders. "Okay, I'm not licensed to sell this alcoholic beverage to you," he said, pointing to the unlabeled cider bottles. "Instead, I'll sell you these fine apples"—he handed us two with a wink—"for three euro apiece, and give you two bottles of cider as a gift. D'ya understand?" We did, and the cider was delicious.

The last kilometer of the road out to Galley Head is winding, narrow, and bumpy. It was all the more hazardous because of the distractingly spectacular scenery unfolding in front of us—craggy cliffs pounded by surf from a deep green-blue ocean, perfect blue sky, and pastures of cows outlined by miles of stone walls built over the centuries to contain the livestock. And of course the lighthouse gradually came into view and grew larger as we approached.

We pulled through the gate to the lighthouse grounds and got out of the car next to the cottages and what turned out to be Gerald's van. The lighthouse loomed over us, stark white against the blue sky, rimmed with bright red railings. Gerald got out of his car, and right away we were struck with the idea that he fit into the color scheme of the light, with his shock-white hair, clear blue eyes and ruddy cheeks.

He noted with pride our expressions of awe and delight at finding ourselves in such a singularly beautiful place. His place. He looked at us with a wry grin and a salty glint in his eye, and simply said: "Welcome to Galley Head."

After so many trips overseas, these are the things we love about visiting small-town Ireland: The local food culture, the history, of course the postcard-perfect landscapes; but most of all, the interaction with the locals who call this magical land their home. We hope this guide helps other travelers discover some of that magic for themselves.

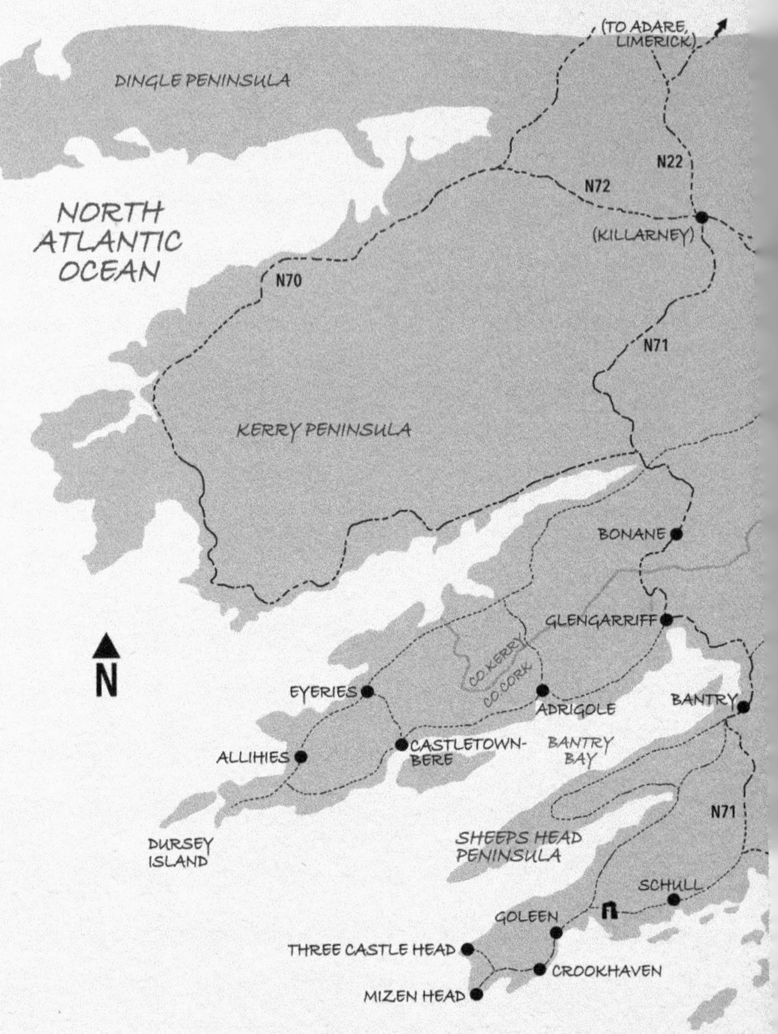

(TO ADARE, LIMERICK)
DINGLE PENINSULA
N22
N72
NORTH ATLANTIC OCEAN
(KILLARNEY)
N70
N71
KERRY PENINSULA
BONANE
GLENGARRIFF
N
CO. KERRY
CO. CORK
EYERIES
ADRIGOLE
BANTRY
CASTLETOWN-BERE
BANTRY BAY
ALLIHIES
N71
SHEEPS HEAD PENINSULA
DURSEY ISLAND
SCHULL
GOLEEN
THREE CASTLE HEAD
CROOKHAVEN
MIZEN HEAD

ROUTE #1

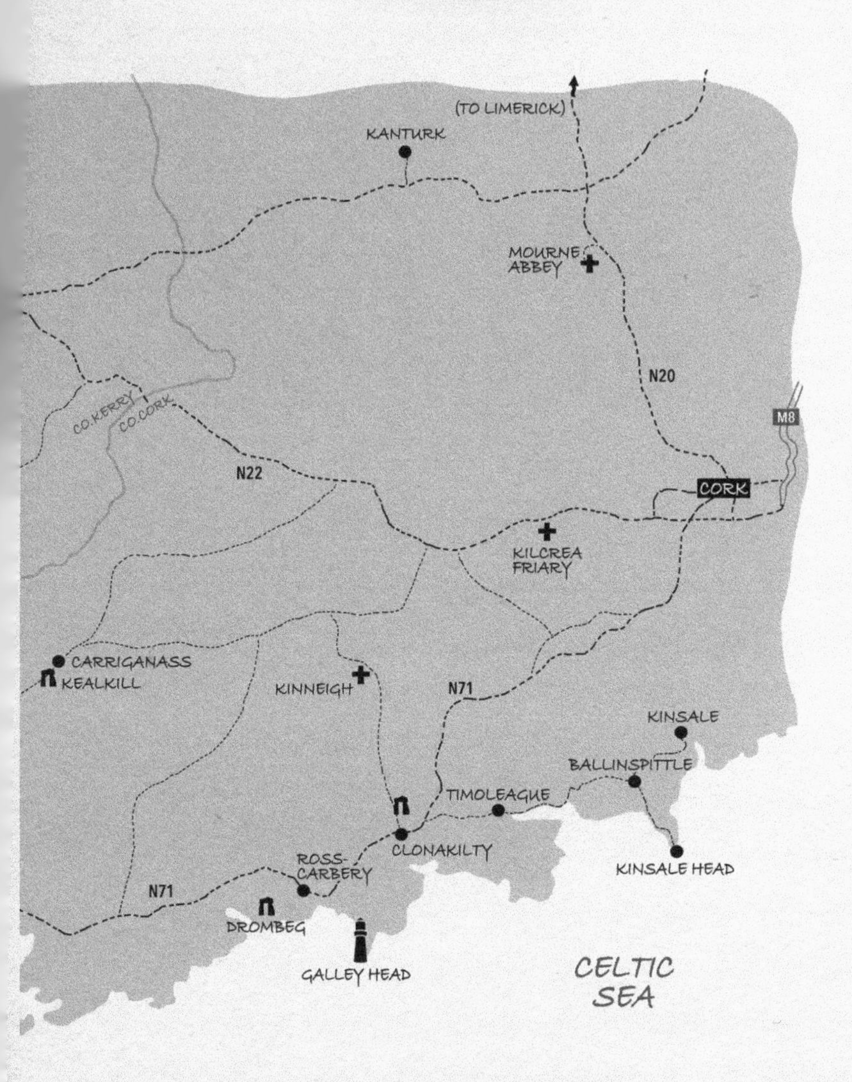
(TO LIMERICK)
KANTURK
MOURNE ABBEY
N20
M8
CO.KERRY
CO.CORK
N22
CORK
KILCREA FRIARY
CARRIGANASS
KEALKILL
KINNEIGH
N71
KINSALE
BALLINSPITTLE
TIMOLEAGUE
CLONAKILTY
KINSALE HEAD
ROSS-CARBERY
N71
DROMBEG
GALLEY HEAD
CELTIC SEA

Southwestern Ireland

County Cork and Vicinity

This itinerary begins in County Cork, Ireland's southernmost region and a cultural entity unto itself. Most people are familiar with Cork as the home of the Blarney Stone, but the county is also a food-lover's paradise, full of postcard-perfect lighthouses, rolling green fields, and quaint, colorful fishing villages. This is where the U.S. was drawn into World War I, where Jimi Hendrix's bass player retired, and where pubs serve Murphy's Stout rather than Guinness.

Driving out from Cork town, you'll find that the region has many opportunities to follow the "brown signs", which are road markers leading to historical sites throughout the countryside. To the west, look for Abbey Road (just a street name, not a Beatles reference) south from the N22. This leads to a walk through the extensive grounds and thick stone walls of the 15th-century **Kilcrea Friary**. To the north, just off the N20 near Ballynamona, stand the ghostly ruins of **Mourne Abbey**. Built in 1199, supposedly by the Knights Templar, it was "suppressed" (that is, raided, looted, and destroyed) by the forces of Henry VIII in the 1540s; it's now overtaken by ivy and cows. Farther north and west, the splendid shell of **Kanturk Castle** is open to passers-by directly on the road south of Kanturk town—an open-air testament to the wealth and power of the lords of past ages, now home only to crows. Sites such as these abound throughout Ireland—medieval monuments that are free to visit.

To the west is County Kerry, and its famous sights: the Dingle peninsula, Killarney National Park, and the much-traveled Ring of Kerry. Many Ireland guides thoroughly cover these (undeniably beautiful) areas. After you've had your fill of bumper-to-bumper traffic, road-hogging buses, and crowded tourist attractions, try instead the following less-traveled alternatives.

To the south of the Ring of Kerry is the Beara peninsula, which juts out into the Atlantic between the bays of Kenmare and Bantry. On the way down, you'll pass the unassuming little shop of **Lorge Chocolatiers** on the N71, in an old post office building in Bonane. Here you will find the French-born Benoit Lorge creating finest-quality handmade chocolates in-house.

Continue on toward Bantry Bay to **Glengarriff**, a small one-street town in a prime location. Take the passenger ferry across the town harbor to **Garnish Island**; on the ride you'll pass clusters of seals stretched out on the rocky protrusions. The island was a military outpost in the Napoleonic wars. Its squat Martello tower dates

from 1805, when the island was stripped bare for strategic reasons. The aristocratic Bryce family took over Garnish in the early 1900s and turned it into a sub-tropical garden paradise. It sits on a sweet spot of the Atlantic gulf stream, giving it an unusual climate suitable for growing all manner of flora—plants grow nearly twice as fast here than elsewhere in Ireland.

In town, the **Glengarriff Park Hotel** is well-situated, comfortable, and affordable; its attached eateries (the **Park Bistro** and **MacCarthy's Pub**) offer a nice mix of modern fare and traditional pub dishes. For a bit of variety, walk to the other end of town (a mere 100 yards or so) to **Casey's**, a restaurant and hotel that specializes in serving local seafood dishes. Casey's is a family-run, friendly place. This is a good place to get some Bantry Bay mussels, regarded across the county as the best.

Glengarriff also serves as the gateway to the "**Ring of Beara**", a drive around the peninsula that rivals that of Kerry in all but its volume of traffic. On this circuit you'll see countless medieval sites and stone-age megaliths—we include just a few of our favorites here, but it would be easy to spend several days here and still not see everything. (To see them all, be on the lookout for those brown sign markers.) This route also has an assortment of brightly colored villages and the occasional artist's shop. Our favorite is the **Hungry Hill Gallery** in the **Adrigole Arts Centre**, an extensive arts shop located just south of Adrigole on the R572. It features artworks by many local artists, and the bottom level has an extensive assortment of crafts from all over Ireland, including pottery, jewelry, soaps, wool sweaters, hats and scarves, and even perfume from the famous Burren Perfumery (which we'll visit in the next itinerary). The gallery also has a nice coffee shop attached, so grab an espresso or latte and a snack to spur you along on your drive.

In the town of Castletown-Bearhaven (often shortened to "Castletownbere"), bear right at the "Olde Bakery" and follow signs for the **Derreenataggart stone circle**, one of our favorite sites on Beara: a large and mostly intact circle of nine stones (plus three more that have fallen), overlooking the valley below and its surrounding foothills. Be careful: The stones are sometimes heavily guarded... by cows. (And when the cows retreat, it's important to watch your step!)

Following the R572 west towards the end of the peninsula, you'll come to a hard left turn towards

Dursey Island. (Going straight, the route becomes R575.) Dursey is a good-sized island just off the coast; its surrounding currents are too dangerous for watercraft, so it's only accessible by a small cable car dangling across the chasm between two cliffs. Photographers, hikers, and wildlife enthusiasts may want to take the time to explore this island, as it doesn't get much more remote than this.

Directly at the 572/575 junction, there's a field to the left. Here stands the **Killaugh wedge grave**. This is a typical burial structure of the Neolithic period—a huge slab supported at an angle by smaller upright slabs. It's worth appreciating that the Irish people built their roads with reverence to sites like this, despite the fact that it appears at first glance to be little more than a sunken pile of rocks. The Irish had—and still have—a great reverence for the pre-history of ancient Eire.

Continuing on the R575, you'll come to the colorful little village of **Allihies**. Just before the town, look for a sign to the **Children of Lir Mythic Site**. A small boulder commemorates the Irish legend in which four children of King Lir were turned into swans by his jealous second wife, who consigned them to 900 years of living in the Irish countryside lakes and coastal marshes. Visitors leave coins on the stone, presumably as a sort of wishing-well tradition. Allihies is also home to a museum of copper mining, preserving an important part of the real history of the region.

The R575 road meets up with the R571. A right turn here leads south across the mountains of the peninsula back to Castletownbere; a left will take you to some inviting beaches on the north coast, and then to **Eyeries**. Fred Astaire fans may recognize this town and its surroundings as the location of his 1977 film *The Purple Taxi*. Like Allihies, Eyeries is rainbow-painted, and has a few pubs, shops, and eateries.

Follow the side road that parallels the R571 through Eyeries to stay on the Ring of Beara route. Look for signs to the **Hag of Beara**, another ancient site attached to mythical lore. This is purportedly the stone face of a demigoddess of the pagan pantheon, who was petrified by a Christian saint when she tried to quell his efforts to spread the "new religion" in Ireland. The face is in profile and looks out over the water.

Just a little farther on is **Kilcatherine Cemetery**, which surrounds a ruined church dating from the 7th century AD. The gravestones here span centuries, including many that are no more than anonymous slabs sticking out of the ground. One particularly ancient and mysterious marker is a weathered cross cut from a single stone. Several of the church's arched doors and windows remain intact. There is also a curious cat's head carved into one rock protrusion, possibly a nod to the old religion of the land before Christianity co-opted most of Ireland's sacred sites.

Returning to the R571, continue east to Ardgroom. Just past the town is a turnoff to the south for the **Ardgroom stone circle**. This one is quite striking for its panoramic position on the hillside. It requires a bit of hiking through a couple of fields, so again, watch your step. Nine stones are still standing, though it likely had eleven originally. A single standing stone watches over the circle a short distance away. The isolation here amongst these ancient stone formations creates a magical atmosphere.

Upon reaching Lauragh, you can continue following the Beara route into County Kerry, or turn right down the R574 and up through the **Healy Pass**. This route was built in 1847 to improve area transportation during the famine years. Look down over the hills as you climb and you'll see ribbons of waterfalls streaming down the rocks to feed small lakes. It's easy to imagine the Children of Lir swans residing in one of these before returning to their original state. This stretch is a gorgeous drive, a winding road climbing up rocky gorges past intrepid goats, and yet never more than a couple of miles from the coast.

From Glengarriff, go south on the N71, and then divert northeast on the R584. This leads to **Kealkill**, the site of a hilltop stone circle by the same name. Nearby on the riverside is **Carriganass Castle**. Built in the 1540s and home of the once powerful O'Sullivan Beare clan, this tower house is now a waypoint on several different walking paths and pilgrimage routes. It was also the site of one of the exploits of the legendary (and almost certainly fictitious) folk hero Donal Cam

who infiltrated the castle and threw his wife's murderer from the tower into the river below.

Continuing on the N71 you'll reach the large, bustling port town of **Bantry** at the tail end of Bantry Bay, the source of the prized eponymous mussels. Bantry has countless pubs, restaurants, hotels, and shops. Our favorite is right on the N71, **The Craft Shop**, which offers carefully curated art and craftworks from artisans all over Ireland, and has been in business for over 40 years. Two doors down the street is an excellent eatery and food shop, **Organico**, offering organic baked goods, sandwiches, salads, coffee and tea... plenty of goodies to sustain you on your next leg of your journey.

Proceed south to Mizen Peninsula, which reaches the southernmost point of Ireland. Smaller than Beara, the Mizen juts out into the Atlantic with similarly angled cliffs and rocky shoals interrupted here and there by soft, white sand beaches. Head south and west on the R592 to

Schull (pronounced, and sometimes spelled, "Skull"), a little harbor town with a lot of charm. Here, of course, seafood is paramount to the economy and the cuisine. The **Bunratty Inn** at the top of Main Street is a good place to stop for a pint and a dish of seafood chowder; they offer pub food that incorporates local foodstuffs like the delicious cheese from nearby **Gubbeen dairy farm**. Schull also has a weekly food market near the pier on Sundays, where local farmers and other food vendors sell their goods–fruits and vegetables, jams and sauces, meats, breads and other bakery treats, cheeses, and of course fish, as well as a variety of crafts such as woodworking, pottery, knitwear, glass art, and jewelry.

On Seafood Chowder...

"No matter where y'are in Ireland," a barkeep once told us, "y're never far from the coast, are ya?" It wasn't a question; it was a statement of fact. A fact that leads to a corollary: Especially in places directly on the Irish coast, seafood chowder is a prized menu item—usually made in-house, and with fresh fish from the local fish-monger. (It's always good to ask if they make their own, even though they may think you're daft for supposing it could be otherwise.) It's a cream-based soup, ranging from brothy to cement-mixer-thick, made with potatoes and vegetables. The main ingredients, of course, are the fish: Mussels, shrimp, various pieces of whitefish and salmon, maybe scallops or clams or crab, or even oyster or squid. The specific fish depends on what's seasonal and typical in the area. You'll know you're eating what the locals are eating—and in some cases, what they themselves caught that day.

Proceed west on the R592, or on the parallel side roads that more closely hug the water's edge. In just a few kilometers, a 4000-year-old megalith called an "**Altar Wedge Tomb**" stands on the side of the road overlooking the Toormore Bay. As it has a much larger flat platform than other wedge tombs, this monument has developed a reputation not just as an ancient burial place (which archaeologists confirm) but also as the site of ritual human sacrifice by pre-Christian druids. There's no evidence that this or any other such site was ever actually used for human sacrifice though; it was probably a legend cooked up later on in order to discredit and demonize the old religion in favor of the new. Later in history, Catholics would gather here surreptitiously to hold mass when it was illegal to do so. This is an unusual Stone Age construction, perhaps befitting the prominence of the people buried therein and its singular position on the coast.

The R592 ends in Toormore. Here, pick up the R591 to Goleen, where the **Heron's Cove Bed & Breakfast and Restaurant** is a perfect location to stay comfortably, eat well, and explore this part of the county. It's right on a little protected sea cove; and yes, there are herons that hang out there, whom you can watch from one of the balcony rooms or the restaurant's patio.

Proceed farther west and make your winding

way to **Crookhaven**. Just before coming into town, you'll see the **Church of Saint Brendan the Navigator**, a Protestant church (uncommon in Ireland) that was built in 1717 on the remains of a much older church. Like many churches in Ireland (and Irish-founded churches elsewhere), it is dedicated to Brendan, coastal Ireland's most popular saint, an intrepid Odysseus-like figure from the 5th and 6th centuries.

A sleepy fishing village tucked in a "crook" in the land forming a protected harbor, Crookhaven is a fantastic location from which to explore this little corner of Ireland. This was historically a last port of call for ships provisioning themselves before setting out for the Americas.

Jorg's Goldsmith Studio, on the main strip, offers fine handcrafted jewelry (made by Jorg himself right there in the studio), as well as selling other crafts from other artists. Next door is the

Crookhaven Inn, the first place outside of Italy that we designated a "destination restaurant". From its hearty, seeded, nutty brown bread

(baked fresh every few hours), to its mouthwatering treatments of Bantry mussels, to its perfectly seared fish fresh from the boats outside the front door, the food here is a fantastic combination of local ingredients, high-quality preparation, and comfortable atmosphere.

Irish brown soda bread

Almost without exception, any meal you get in an Irish eatery will be served with an abundance of Irish brown soda bread. Since the advent of bicarbonate of soda in the 19th century, this iconic recipe has been a staple throughout Ireland. A dense, hearty bread, made quickly and with simple ingredients, hits the spot after a hard day on the fishing trawler or out in the pastures. It's also the perfect tool for soaking up the ends of your chowder or enjoying a bit too much delicious Irish butter. It comes in all shapes and sizes, from little biscuits to large loaves with a cross cut into the top (to bless the bread, of course!).

The many rocky crags and crooked coastline of the Mizen peninsula (and indeed on most of Ireland's Atlantic coast) necessitates guidance for ships. There are consequently many lighthouses marking the way. Following the road farther west and south, you'll arrive finally at **Mizen Head Signal Station**, the lighthouse at the southernmost tip of contiguous Ireland. The visitors' center here is now a tourist attraction, however remote. A museum displays the history of the area and the lives of the keepers of the lights over the centuries. The lighthouse itself sits on a little cliff island separated by a gorge. Visitors paying admission to the museum grounds can cross a dizzying footbridge over the chasm to gain access to the tower and get a glimpse of the seemingly infinite reaches of the ocean.

This site can be crowded, compared to the relative isolation of the rest of Mizen. The views here are certainly spectacular, so you'll have to decide for yourself if the costs and the crowds are worth it. Best to avoid the place in the summer, unless you arrive early in the day. Even if you don't pay to go into the lighthouse grounds, this point offers great views just from the parking lot: Look to the southeast for the distant **Fastnet Rock lighthouse**, a 19th-century signal light built far out into the ocean on a lonely rock protrusion—it looks like

something out of a fantasy tale.

An alternative is to seek out **Three-Castle Head**, on the westernmost point of the peninsula to the north of the Mizen Station point. Though accessible only after a considerable (30+ minutes) hike from the nearest road, the location is absolutely worth the time and effort. After crossing grassy farmers' fields, passing through or over several stone pasture walls, and ascending a rocky hillside path, the intrepid traveler is suddenly and breathtakingly rewarded with magical views of Dun Lough, a little lake surrounded by craggy mountains right by the coast. Here also stand the ghostly ruins of a medieval castle and tower house, built in the 15th century by the prominent (and, judging by the location, perhaps antisocial) O'Mahoney clan, who retreated here from Norman invaders. Arrive early in the day for the best chance of being here alone, and you'll feel like you've discovered a secret, enchanted vale.

Returning east, the N71 leads along the southern coast, part of the signposted Wild Atlantic Way drive. You'll eventually come to **Clonakilty**, a colorful and bustling harbor town within easy distance of a wealth of sights. The town itself has a few not-to-be-missed food stops: **DeBarra's** serves solid pub fare (ask for Murphy's, not Guinness!), and is famous for its live music. Memorabilia on several walls remember Noel Redding, Jimi

Hendrix's original bass player, who lived and played here for the last quarter-century of his life. Around the corner is the **Lettercollum Kitchen Project**, a multifaceted food shop: The folks here sell goods from local producers (such as delicious

smoked fish from Woodcock Smokery), and they produce herbs and vegetables from their own nearby gardens. They make all sorts of dishes in-house, the ultimate in farm-to-table fare; and in the spring and summer they offer gardening/cooking classes.

Weekly town markets and Farm shops

One of the best places to find locally sourced, organic, and sustainably-raised foodstuffs in Ireland is at weekly town markets. Each town holds their market on a different day of the week, when you can visit the tents or stalls of local produce-growers, jam-canners, dairy farmers, cheese-makers, livestock-herders, fish-mongers, bread-bakers, and ale-brewers—everything you need to eat and drink for a day (or a week) at a self-catering lodging. Alternatively, many farms have shops, either in town or at the farm itself, where they sell the goods they produce. It's all fresh, and it's crafted or grown by people who really know what they're doing. This is one way to immerse yourself in the local culture, while also being an affordable way to eat healthy, high-quality, and delicious food on your travels.

Across the street from DeBarra's is **Gearoidin's Bakery**, known locally for its cakes and baked goods, as artistic as they are delicious. Next door to Gearoidin's is the historic **Edward Twomey's** butchery, famous since the 1800s for its Clonakilty Blackpudding. When the butchery was passed on to Edward Twomey in the 1970s, he decided to cease producing the iconic product, but public outcry was so fierce that he relented and continues the tradition of making this vital staple of County Cork's breakfast tables. Today the recipe is unchanged from its roots in the 19th century. If you're In Clonakilty on a Friday, it's market day, and you can stock up on fresh local produce and more. Look for the apple guy, who sells apples, juice, and bottles of delicious cider.

Southeast of Clonakilty on the Old Timoleague Way, grab a memorable lunch at the **Deasy's Harbour Bar and Seafood Restaurant**. Deasy's bakes their own delicious breads, and uses the bounty of the local fishermen (you'll see some of them at their boats moored across the street) as well as creative use of other local products to create delicious starters and mains. The menu changes daily depending on what's fresh at the market. If it's "on", try their Irish onion soup—a locally sourced take on the more well known French variety.

Continuing east along the Wild Atlantic Way route leads to the colorful **Timoleague**, prominent for its spooky abbey ruins. Founded in 1240 AD and built on a 6th-century monastic settlement, **Timoleague Friary** sits at the edge of this small bayside town. It consists of an extensive set of buildings—including the wall, church rooms, a cemetery, and a tower—that visitors are free to wander at will. At this and a few other such sites, you'll see signs warning against grave-digging—not without proper precautions at least. Also, those affected by warts might want to visit the sacristy and check out the Wart Well, a hollowed-out stone called a "bullaun". If you dip your wart into the well, it is said that it will be healed. (Note: Little Roads Europe is not liable for any infections resulting from doing this.)

For a memorable lunch here, go to **Monk's Lane**, a gastropub popular with the locals. Monk's Lane has an extensive list of wine and craft ales, and serves upscale plates and pub classics with equal skill and taste. They also

offer fresh scones and a wide array of gourmet coffee and tea.

The drive from Timoleague to **Ballinspittle** along the Wild Atlantic Way is one of our favorites. Every turn brings another incredible view of the Atlantic, or a postcard-worthy shot of a painted village, including Ballinspittle itself. Here you'll find **Diva Boutique Bakery and Deli**, which sells imported foodstuffs as well as local products. You can get a latte or cappuccino here, as well as cakes and cookies (including many gluten-free options), high-quality oil and vinegar,

olives, and meats and cheeses, and some of the best sandwiches we've had anywhere. Grab a pint next door at the friendly, family-run Hurley's Bar; or for a sit-down lunch, just down the block is Diva's own café.

On the coast straight south of Ballinspittle, the **Blue Horizon B&B** is perched on a hillside, over-

looking the Irish Sea and the Kinsale Head peninsula to the east. A couple of the rooms have little balconies with views of the landscape—the sea, the rolling pastures, and the peninsula of Kinsale Head.

Kinsale Head is infamous as the site where the Germans sank the Lusitania in 1915, one of the

propulsive events of World War I that drew the United States into the global conflict. The point, with its rocky cliffs supporting broad meadows, includes a 17th-century lighthouse and the ruins of a 2000-year-old stone fort thought to have been built by the Celts. (Unfortunately, the whole peninsula is now a walled, private golf resort, not exactly a fitting memorial to the 1100 people who lost their lives in the event, or the millions who died in the subsequent war.)

To the north of the head, Kinsale itself is a busy river-port town. Just on the other side of the river River Bandon, outside of town, is the **Bulman Bar and Restaurant**, which serves delicious, locally sourced foods. Chances are fair that they'll be able to tell you the names of the fishermen who, that morning, brought in the fish that now sit perfectly cooked on your plate.

Returning to Clonakilty: To the north are a couple of interesting ancient sites. Just outside of town is the **Templebryan Stone Circle**, and nearby the ruins of an early Christian settlement includes an inscribed standing stone and a bullaun stone. Farther north on the R588 is the **Kinneagh Round Tower**, built in the 11th century as part of a monastery, of which St Bartholomew's church and its surrounding graveyard still stand.

The tower is built on a hexagonal base, the only one of its kind in all of Ireland.

To the south of Clonakilty is **Drombeg Stone Circle**, just off the R597 road. Locally known as the Druid's Altar, the circle has 17 stones, including two large portal stones and one "recumbent" stone that may have been an altar or platform. It is thought that recumbent stone circles like this are aligned with various astronomical seasonal events. This one seems to line up with sunset on the winter solstice. Unlike many of these Neolithic sites, Drombeg is well-marked, with easy parking, free access, and an easy path to the circle, so get there early to avoid crowds spoiling the magic. A bit to the east is the colorful little village of **Rosscarbery**. The cute town square is home to quaint storefronts including **Pilgrim's**, a gastropub whose local and seasonal menu changes daily.

Pick up a few snacks in town and head down just a few minutes' drive to **Owenahincha**

Beach, a beautiful stretch of soft sand and round stones. This is one of three beaches in a row here, separated by rocky outcroppings. From here, the Galley Head peninsula and its lighthouse are visible to the southeast. Unless you're a seal (you may see some in the shallows), swimming here is not permitted, as the currents are deadly, but a stroll along the strand or a picnic near the dunes makes a lovely couple of hours.

Despite the swimming prohibition, nice summertime weather could mean big crowds at these beaches. To escape, follow the little roads out to the **Galley Head Lighthouse**. This is not just a postcard-perfect scene, it's also a lodging managed by the Irish Landmark Trust, a nonprofit organization that maintains unique historic properties all over Ireland.

Unlike the other (nearly a dozen) Irish lighthouses that are available for lodging, Galley Head's keeper Gerald Butler visits the site regularly. If your timing is good, Gerald, a third-generation lightkeeper, will give you a tour of the lighthouse itself. The two keepers' cottages are well-appointed holiday apartments, with complete kitchens and turf-burning fireplaces. Before your stay here, a thoughtful gathering of supplies at the various aforementioned food vendors can make this a magical and unique experience. Cook local eggs and fresh bread for breakfast (don't

forget the black pudding!), then take a mug of coffee or tea out to walk the perimeter of the lighthouse grounds and enjoy the smell of the Irish Sea, the sound of the surf on the cliffs and the seabirds calling, and the boundless views in all directions. Look for pods of dolphins as they leap their way along the coast. If you're lucky you may even spot a whale. Watch the distant fishing boats, working to bring the day's catch to the local market. Savor a lunch of smoked mackerel and local greens with a couple of glasses of cider made at the nearby orchards. Finish off with a sweet treat from one of the excellent bakers in the area. Then toss back a couple of Murphy's with your dinner before curling up in front of the fireplace with your favorite book—or your favorite person.

Restaurants are open every day for lunch and dinner unless otherwise noted.

Glengarriff

Casey's

Family-run restaurant that always has local produce and seafood on the menu. If you are a fisherman, the restaurant will cook your catch for you at the end of the day! This place is also a hotel, with huge, fluffy beds. Friendly, family-run place.

http://www.caseyshotelglengarriff.ie/

Crookhaven

The Crookhaven Inn

Stunning, gorgeous food, nearly everything made in house. Inventive use of local, seasonal ingredients – with the influence of international tastes. Open every day for lunch and dinner, but closed October - Easter. Reservations recommended.

http://www.thecrookhaveninn.com/

Clonakilty

DeBarra's Folk Club

This pub is famous for its music (and music history), but we had the best fish and chips we've ever eaten here. This is also a good place to try the famous Clonakilty Black Pudding, made just across the street. Open Monday - Saturday for lunch from 12 - 4. Pub open every day till midnight.

http://debarra.ie/

Gearoidin's Bakery

Cozy, small cafe serving lunch, early dinners, and well known for their excellent desserts. Great place to grab a to-go coffee and baked treat.

Open Monday - Saturday 9:30 - 6, Sunday 11 - 5.

Deasy's Harbour Bar and Seafood Restaurant

Incredible food in an idyllic, remote location right on the harbor, just a few minutes drive from Clonakilty town. Everything made in-house. Open Wednesday-Sunday for dinner, Saturday and Sunday also open for light lunches. Call for reservations: 023-88-35741

Rosscarbery

Pilgrim's

Upscale but homey restaurant in the cute little town of Rosscarbery. Menu is quite small as everything is handmade; the menu changes daily based on what is at the market. Open for dinner Wednesday - Saturday, 6 - 10pm; Sunday lunch 1 - 4 pm.

http://pilgrims.ie/

Timoleague

Monk's Lane

Adorable gastropub on the Wild Atlantic Way serving locally sourced food. Excellent wine list and craft beer and cider selection.Front room is impossibly cute with fresh flowers and candles on the tables.

Closed most of January, and Mondays and Tuesdays. Food served Wednesday - Saturday 12:30 - 3 and 6 -9, bar open all day. Open Sunday 1 - 7.

http://monkslane.ie/

Kinsale

The Bulman Pub

Excellent gastropub just 10 meters from the sea, serving fish caught just outside their front door. Reservations recommended as this place is extremely popular. Open for lunch every day from 1 - 5. Dinner Tuesday - Saturday from 6 - 9.

http://www.thebulman.ie/

Ballinspittle

Diva Boutique Bakery and Cafe

Funky little cafe and shop offering freshly baked bread and desserts, and lunch items like sandwiches and soups. Loads of gluten free options. Great place to pick up a cappuccino and cake. Diva's has two locations, across the street from each other: a shop, and a sit-down cafe. The place has some of the best pastries we've had in all Ireland.

Open Wednesday - Saturday 9:30 - 5, Sunday 11 - 5. Closed for winter break January - mid March.

http://divaboutiquebakery.com/

Glengarriff

Casey's Hotel (see listing above in Where to Eat)

Glengarriff Park Hotel

Boutique hotel in the center of the village of Glengarriff. Comfortable, plush beds. Great food downstairs at The Park Bistro, or traditional pub fare at MacCarthy's Bar – both places owned by the hotel.

Double rooms from 56€.

http://glengarriffpark.com/

Galley Head

Galley Head Lighthouse

The lighthouse-keeper's cottages at Galley Head have been transformed into beautiful vacation rentals. Full kitchen, open fire, unbeatably gorgeous location.

2-night stay minimum, but given the location we recommend you stay longer.

From 400€ for 2 nights.

http://www.irishlandmark.com/

Goleen

The Heron's Cove Restaurant & Bed and Breakfast

A cute B&B and restaurant with gorgeous views of the harbor. Remote and serene. Rooms 2 through 5 share a balcony overlooking the harbor. Communal patio overlooking the harbor for the use of all guests. Restaurant serves dinners with locally-caught fish every night from May - September. Reservations for dinner are necessary. B&B is open year-round; restaurant open Saturday nights. From 70€ for a double room. Excellent Full Irish breakfast in the morning.

http://www.heronscove.com/

Garrettstown

The Blue Horizon B&B

On the Wild Atlantic Way, about a 10 minute drive from Kinsale. We recommend Room 15, which is a triple, because the room has gorgeous picture windows with views of the countryside and ocean. Hosts Mary and Jimmy are welcoming and friendly. Self catering apartments downstairs. Guests can request a pint of Murphy's from the bar, which is closed to the public. Full Irish breakfast cooked to order in the morning.

Triple room from 108€, other rooms for less.

http://www.thebluehorizon.com/

Sights are free to enter unless otherwise noted. Kilcrea Friary, Mourne Abbey, Kanturk Castle, Ring of Beara, Derreenataggart stone circle, Children of Lir mythic site, Hag of Beara, Kilcatherine Cemetery, Healy Pass, Carriganass Castle, Altar wedge tomb, Church of Saint Brendan the Navigator, Timoleague Friary, Templebryan stone circle, Kinneagh round tower, Drombeg stone circle, Owenahincha beach.

Glengarriff

Garnish Island

Take the 10€ ferry ride, viewing harbor seals along the way, to visit this idyllic island with Italianate gardens, formal gardens, the Martello tower, and take a tour of Bryce House, where Agatha Christie and George Bernard Shaw stayed and wrote. A guided tour of the house takes 45 minutes.

Entry to island: 5€. Hours vary by season, check website for full details.

http://www.garnishisland.com/

Mizen Peninsula

Three Castle Head

Absolutely stunning castle ruins, tucked away in a valley, about a 30 minute walk from the road. There is a farmhouse and cafe here, open in the summertime. The walk is signposted along the way. Absolutely worth the effort to get here, one of our most favorite places in Ireland. The visit is free but there is a suggested 3€ donation; we suggest donating a bit more to maintain the site.

http://www.threecastlehead.ie/

Bonane

Lorge Chocolatiers

Handmade chocolates created by French chef Benoit Lorge, using fine ingredients sourced from around the world. Chef makes multiple varieties of marzipan as well, the best we have had anywhere.

Open every day 10 - 6.

http://lorge.ie/

Ring of Beara

Adrigole Arts and Hungry Hill Gallery

A lovely shop carrying an impressive collection of works by artisans from all over Ireland: jewelry, ceramics, woolen goods, soaps, perfumes, crafts. The Hungry Hill gallery upstairs displays contemporary artworks by Irish artists. There is a cafe here as well where you can get a great coffee.

Cafe open Easter - October.

Shop open year round 10 -6, but call ahead if you plan to visit January - March. +353 - 27 60234

https://www.facebook.com/Adrigole-Arts-612925078780999/?ref=br_rs

Crookhaven

Jorg's Goldsmith Studio

Handmade gold and silver jewelry, crafted onsite in studio by goldsmith Jorg Uschkamp.

Open every day in summer, and most days in shoulder seasons. Call or write ahead in shoulder and off seasons to inquire about hours.

http://jorgsgoldsmithstudio.com/

Clonakilty

Lettercollum Kitchen Project

The front is a shop carrying local products like cheese, meat, tea, honey and more; the back is an active kitchen turning out fresh bread, baked goods, and seasonal foods. A perfect place to shop to stock up if you are in a vacation rental, grab some gifts to bring home, or pick up lunch. Classes are offered here as well for more serious foodies

Open Tuesday - Friday 10 - 6; Saturday 10 - 5. Closed Sunday and Monday.

http://www.lettercollum.ie/

Bantry

The Craft Shop Bantry

Lovely craft shop right on the main road in Bantry. This place has been open for over 40 years and is a treasure-trove of crafts made by artisans all over Ireland. Ceramics, handmade leather shoes and belts, jewelry, candles, soaps....there is something here for every budget. Open 10 - 6 Monday through Saturday. Closed Sunday, and also Wednesdays in winter.

https://www.craftshopbantry.com/

Organico

On the N71, just two doors down from The Craft Shop. Health food store with full grocery, and a popular bustling cafe where you can find delicious sandwiches, baked goods, soups, and coffee (also to-go).

Open Monday - Saturday 9 - 6.

https://www.organico.ie

ROUTE #2

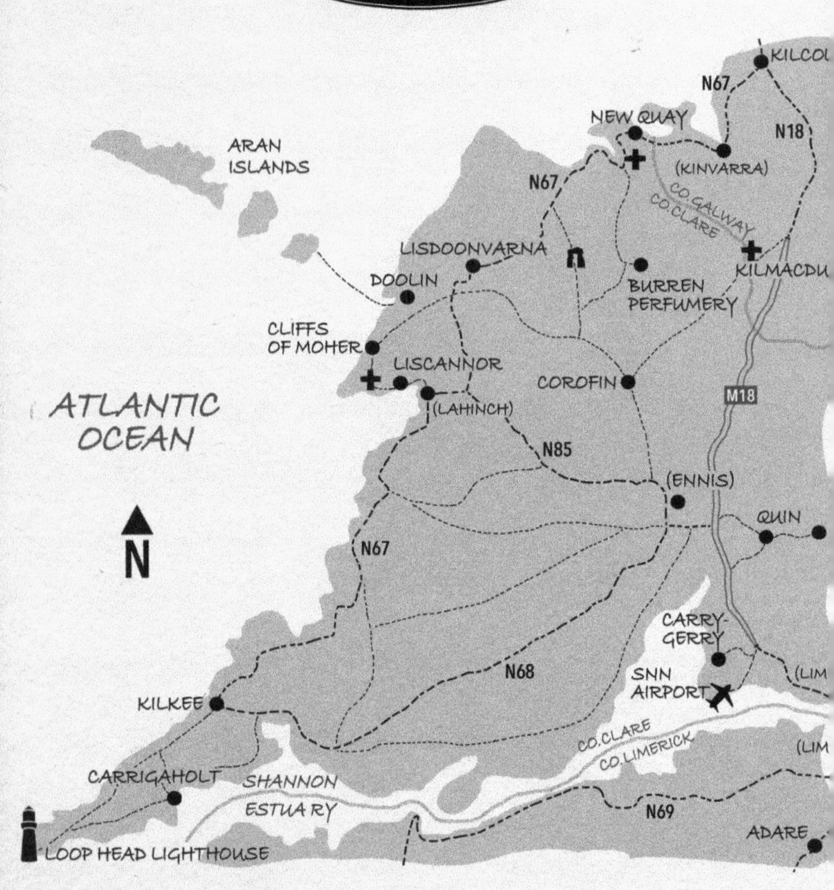

ARAN ISLANDS
NEW QUAY
N67
N18
(KINVARRA)
CO.GALWAY
CO.CLARE
LISDOONVARNA
DOOLIN
BURREN PERFUMERY
KILMACDU
CLIFFS OF MOHER
LISCANNOR
COROFIN
(LAHINCH)
M18
ATLANTIC OCEAN
N85
(ENNIS)
QUIN
N
N67
CARRY-GERRY
N68
SNN AIRPORT
KILKEE
CO.CLARE
CO.LIMERICK
CARRIGAHOLT
SHANNON ESTUARY
N69
ADARE
LOOP HEAD LIGHTHOUSE

Western Ireland

County Clare and Vicinity

This itinerary leads to the fabled and towering Cliffs of Moher—and to another equally breathtaking, tourist-free alternative. Visit "Ireland's prettiest village"; take in the tunes in western Ireland's "music town"; and explore the stark landscape of a geological oddity, the rocky and beautiful Burren. County Clare includes Shannon Airport, which receives a lot of air traffic from the U.S. A large number of visitors coming into the west of Ireland therefore make this their first area to visit.

Approaching County Clare from the south, you'll come to the town of **Adare**, a bit south of Limerick town. The bridge at Adare was historically the only crossing of the River Maigue for many miles, so it became a major waypoint of commerce and travel. Several monasteries were founded here in medieval times. Unlike many of the abbeys listed in this guide, these have been updated and are still in use today.

The town is designated as a "Heritage Town of Ireland" for its history and well-preserved architecture. The town's own visitors bureau calls it "Ireland's prettiest village", and it just might be: Its colorful street fronts, its medieval architecture, its city park, its dovecote, and its rows of thatch-roofed cottages certainly make it a candidate for anyone's Top 10 list.

Adare is about a 30-minute drive south of Shannon airport, so it's a good place to lodge before departing from SNN. Our favorite place to stay here is the **Village Inn** on the main N21 road, attached to the **Sean Collins & Sons Bar**. The Collins family has run this establishment since the 1940s. They specialize in excellent steaks from their local butcher, Costello's. In fact, **Brian Costello** himself was in the pub when we checked in.

For quieter and more stately lodging (yet, counter-intuitively, even closer to the airport), try **Carrygerry Country House**. Though just 10 minutes from the airport, you'll feel like you're at an 18th-century country manor house—because it is. Watch thoroughbred horses cavorting, hear cows mooing, and spot rabbits scampering in the fields next to the Shannon estuary, as planes come and go in the distance. In the evening, enjoy a cocktail in the parlour and a fine meal in the conservatory of their award-winning restaurant. In the morning, get started with a traditional Irish breakfast before setting out on the day's travels.

To the north is the town of Quin and the well-preserved 14th-century remains of **Quin Abbey**. Unlike many of these old ruins, this one has a tower that visitors can climb to enjoy views of the countryside. (Note: Unlike in the U.S., visitor sites like these in Ireland are generally not monitored, and have few, if any, safety precautions such as handrails. Be smart, use good judgment, and remember that the place is 700+ years old and made entirely of unyielding stone.)

Across the street from the abbey is the aptly

named **Abbey Tavern Bar & Bistro**, offering modern, high-quality dining in a renovated Victorian-era building. Try their banoffi pie (spellings vary, as this isn't a real word), a caramel toffee dessert with bananas. A restaurateur in England invented the recipe in the 1970s, and it quickly spread worldwide. It's now a common item on Irish dessert menus.

For something a bit more modern, head west to the market town of **Ennis**, on a bend of the River Fergus. The town's name derives from the Irish *Inis*, meaning "island". A 13th-century friary was built on what used to be an island formed by two courses of the river. This is County Clare's biggest town. Its old historic section includes the County Clare museum, the abbey ruins, old churches and picturesque bridges, and many colorful streets full of shops and pubs. For a quiet and comfortable place to escape the bustle, try staying at the homey and cute **Glenomra House B&B** on the edge of town.

Driving north on the N85 and then south (west) on the N67, you'll come to one of Ireland's most famous sites: the grandiose, breathtaking, towering **Cliffs of Moher**. Unfortunately, everyone else is going there too, so be prepared for busloads of crowds, noisy group tours, and lots of selfie-sticks pointing in your face. We'll return to this location in a bit. For now, trust us, and proceed north 10-15 minutes up the coast to **Doolin**.

Doolin is a small but active fishing town, known especially for its music. Many of the pubs have traditional Irish bands playing most nights. **Gus O'Connor's Pub** on Fisher Street offers traditional pub fare and fresh seafood in an old-timey atmosphere. Along this strip is also an interesting little storefront, **Doolin Dinghy Books**, a combination art gallery/bookstore/craft shop.

Traditional music

As musicians ourselves, we rarely seek out musical entertainment in our leisure time. But there's nothing that makes you feel more like you're immersed in the Irish experience than sitting in a small-town pub in front of a fire on a cold night, enjoying a pint of stout and listening to some local musicians play traditional Irish music, or "trad" as they say. Sometimes it's a band; more often it's just an assortment of whatever musicians showed up that night. Either way, this makes for an evening of fun and good *craic*.

A short walk down Fisher Street (or an even shorter drive) leads to the Doolin harbor. From this road, ambitious hikers can find a footpath that leads south along the coast all the way to the Cliffs of Moher. At the pier, fishing boats come and go regularly, as does the local friend of the town, Dusty the Dolphin—you may see her swimming around in the harbor on a nice day. This is also the ferry access to the Aran Islands, another popular tourist destination. These three islands are the traditional home of Aran wool sheep, from which are made the fine woolen products sold in every other storefront in Clare and beyond. (Beware of imposters though. You get what you pay for!)

Doolin has a lot of places to stay. Our favorite is the **Twin Peaks B&B**, a few minutes' walk up the hill from O'Connor's. Innkeepers Pascal and Sinead offer perfect and cozy rooms here, as well as a delicious full Irish breakfast.

Here's how we visited the area from our lodging in Doolin: We arose at 4 am, an hour before dawn, and drove out to the Cliffs of Moher well before sunrise. The parking lot is free and empty at this hour. We walked up to the yawning chasm at the top of the cliffs and stood in absolute solitude. Was it a bit chilly? Well, yes. Windy? Hell, yes. But as the sun began to color the sky purple, pink, and crimson, and the cliffs took on more definition, it was a magical hour. Afterward we got back in the car, returned to the inn and slept another hour or two before arising for breakfast.

For equally stunning cliff views at a more civi-

lized hour, try following the R478 road south out of Doolin, past the 16th-century Doonagore Castle coastal tower house, just south of town; past the **Clare Jam Company** (you may want to stop here and pick up a jar or two of local homemade goodies); past the famous cliffs and the tour buses. Not long after the cliffs you'll come to **St Bridget's Well**, outside Liscannor. This is one of countless sites in Ireland honoring the venerated Irish saint, at the site of a holy well. Pilgrims include this well in their religious wanderings, leaving offerings and, presumably, drawing a blessing from the waters here.

There's not much in the seaside village of **Liscannor**, but you'll want to check out **Vaughan's Anchor Inn**, a family-run gastropub and lodging house that triples as a grocery store. Come for

the excellent seafood and pints of Guinness, stay for the comfortable rooms upstairs. Guests are welcomed with a little basket of homemade chocolate chip cookies and tea. They also serve a remarkable breakfast, including their own raspberry jam and "roses" of smoked salmon. Like Doolin, Liscannor is a popular location from which to visit the Cliffs of Moher.

From Liscannor, keep following the R478 across the Inagh River to Lahinch. From here, take the bigger N67 south, passing through lots of little towns with fun names: Quilty. Craggaknock. Kilkee. This last is a busy resort town, but press on through past the beach and look for brown signs (always the brown signs!) for **Loop Head Drive**.

This is the coastal drive that runs the along the northern edge of the Loop Head Peninsula. This road offers mile after mile of spectacular geology: craggy coastline and dizzying heights. The cliffs here don't reach quite as high as the Cliffs of Moher, but they're just as beautiful, and they'll just as surely kill you if you get careless with your panoramic selfies. Best yet: no buses, no crowds, no admission fee. (Note: The authors of this guide are not responsible for the outcome of taking panoramic selfies on the cliffs.)

This drive is breathtaking. On a clear day, the color of the water varies from vivid turquoise to sea-green to an unearthly deep blue. The waves at the shoreline below crash and spray against house-sized chunks of rock, huge pieces of the cliff that could no longer hold on after eons of wind and surf.

The little cliff road eventually hooks up with the marginally larger R487 (again!) to reach the end of the road at the point of the peninsula. Here, **Loop Head Lighthouse** has stood watch since 1854, assisting ships navigating the treacherous and rocks of the Atlantic coast.

The lighthouse is another Irish Landmark Trust location. As such, it's available as a holiday lodging as well. Stock up in Kilkee, or one of the other little towns on the way, on essentials such as bread, milk, cheese, tea, sausages, eggs, coffee, cider, stout, whiskey. Some careful planning can set you up for a lovely few days of relaxing on the cliff's edge, watching pods of dolphins traversing the waters below, looking down—yes, down—on the aerial acrobatics of sea birds swooping in the ocean winds.

Lighthouses

The Irish coast is dotted with lighthouses, most dating from the 18th-19th centuries in the heyday of British domination of the seas. These lights provided crucial guidance to the ships that navigated the treacherous coastlines. Each lighthouse has a unique blinking pattern—shipmasters had to (and still have to) know these codes, so they could identify which particular rocky shoals or shallow beachheads were ahead. Today all of these lights are electric, and mostly automated. They were originally lit up by lamp oil from whales or other such unfortunate sources.

The southern coastal road of the peninsula leads back east to the Shannon Estuary, the natural harbor fed by the River Shannon. On the way, fishing villages such as Carrigaholt offer dolphin-watching tour boats. Here you'll also find the 15th-century **Carrigaholt Castle**, one of many coastal tower fortifications built for maritime defense in the late Middle Ages. This one was strategically placed at the point where the ocean meets the estuary.

To the east of the cliff coast is a unique geological formation that spans about 1 percent of the entire island of Ireland. Designated as a "Special Conservation Area" by the Irish government, the **Burren National Park** (from the Irish *Boíreann* meaning "rocky place") was formed after a glacier receded at the end of the last ice age, about 10,000 years ago. Geologists will find it a fascinating glacial karst landscape. (It's a long story—almost half a billion years long, actually—and includes lots of caves, underground streams, and a 350-million-year-old tropical sea.) Botanists and zoologists will marvel at the wide array of flora and fauna. Somehow, plants and animals that are normally found either only in tropical climates or only in Alpine environments live side by side in the Burren. The rest of us regular, non-scientific-types will simply be amazed that such a place even exists. Walking the stark limestone "pavement" here feels like a hike on some otherworldly sci-fi moonscape. The park center (based in Corofin, to the south) offers a wealth of information about the place, including guided walks through choice parts of the territory.

In the midst of this weirdly fertile moonscape, look for signs to the **Poulnabrone Dolmen**, off the R480 road south of Ballyvaughan and the touristy Ailwee Cave attraction. Poulnabrone is the most

striking of many prehistoric megaliths in the Burren. It's a chamber tomb—several massive stone slabs propping up an even more massive "capstone"—built around 3500 BC, give or take a century or five. Archaeologists uncovered the remains of more than a dozen Stone Age people who were buried here, once again highlighting the deep spirituality and considerable ingenuity of ancient man.

Not far from here, a few turns down tiny roads lead to the **Burren Perfumery**. A sort of botanical outpost, this shop collects the rare flora of the Burren to create unique soaps and perfumes. Its grounds include a beautifully maintained herb and flower garden, and something tasty is always

cooking in their café. We like this attraction because unlike Poulnabrone (which can be crowded due to ease of access) tour buses aren't permitted down the road to the perfumery, so things stay quiet and peaceful.

At the northwest edge of the Burren area, another small town offers some local color. Once a spa destination in the 19th century due to waters springing from the Burren, the town of **Lisdoonvarna** is now the home of the Matchmaking Festival. From the last week of August to the first week of October, this little village of 800 residents bursts to accommodate some 40,000 visitors who come to enjoy music, eat good food, and find love... or something. Outside of this timeframe, it's easy to book a room at the 1830s Royal Spa Hotel, which retains much of its classic decor and architecture. Outside, follow your nose—the aroma of cooking grains and hops will lead you around the corner to the Roadside Tavern, a bustling and popular brewpub with excellent craft ale and stout on tap. Their "pub-grub" is first-rate, including the best burger we've ever had in Ireland.

Returning north to Ballyvaughan and the N67, proceed east. To the north now is Galway Bay. At Bealaclugga, look for signs leading inland to **Corcomroe Abbey**. This 13th-century ruin, at the northeast edge of the Burren area, was once

known as Sancta Maria de Petra Fertilis ("Saint Mary of the fertile rock"), referring to the rich stone geology of the Burren. The site is one of those places that might make you believe in ghosts (and there are a lot of places like that in Ireland!). The route to the abbey is down a series of little roads, ending in a deserted area surrounded by open farmland and woods. Like many such sites, there is no admission fee, no info center, no restrooms. Just wander through and marvel at the architecture, and try not to get creeped out by the stone tomb effigy of the ancient king who commissioned the place.

Just to the north of the Corcomroe location, look for signs to New Quay, a tiny village on the coast north of the N67, where you'll find **Linnane's Lobster Bar**. Sit here with a meal of fresh seafood (hint: get the lobster, it's kind of their thing) and watch the fishermen unloading their catch on the quay.

Farther along the coast highway you'll cross into County Galway. Just past Kinvarra, you'll see

Dunguaire Castle, a tourist-heavy medieval defensive tower overlooking an inlet of Galway Bay. We prefer instead to head south from Kinvarra about 15 minutes on the little L4508 road to visit the **Kilmacduagh Monastery**. Covering several acres amidst stone-walled pastures, this 11th-century monastic site includes several church ruins, a 13th-century castle house, and the tallest round tower in Ireland. Many of the church spaces and the castle (really just a house for the abbots who lived there centuries ago) are locked, but here's the secret: Knock on the door at the house across the road, where the caretaker lives and runs her farm. Leaving her 5 euros as a deposit gets you the key to the church gates and the castle house, so you can see the atmospheric interiors of these ancient buildings. (You may have to wait a moment, as the caretaker may be busy out back feeding her chickens and cows.)

There's one final, delicious stop before venturing farther into Galway. Just past the tiny town of Kilcolgan, on the river by the same name, you'll find **Moran's Oyster Cottage**. As it's directly on a sea inlet that leads to the bay and then to the Atlantic, Moran's specializes in fresh seafood—"sea-to-table", as they say. This establishment has been in the family since the 18th century, a waypoint for seafarers and land travelers. Stop in for a pint of Guinness, fresh-baked brown bread, and, of course, some Galway Bay oysters, which are regarded as some of the best seafood Ireland has to offer. (They offer delicious grilled oysters as well as raw, for those who prefer not to eat stuff that's still alive.) Moran's encompasses what is so singular about traveling the back roads of Ireland: the history, the territory, and the food connected to it.

Restaurants are open every day for lunch and dinner unless otherwise noted.

Quin

Abbey Tavern Bar & Bistro

Popular with the locals for Sunday lunch. The Tavern is just across the street from the Abbey, so you can enjoy a nice meal after a visit. Stick to the 'mains' menu, which are prepared with more thought and care than the sandwich board. Great homemade Banoffi pie, if you like desserts.

http://www.theabbeytavernquin.com/

Doolin

Gus O'Connor's Pub

Traditional Irish pub, open since 1832,in the small coastal town of Doolin. Well known locally for its food, which is often sourced locally. Excellent Irish coffees. Live traditional Irish music every night from late February-late November.

https://www.gusoconnorspubdoolin.net/

Kilcolgan

Moran's Oyster Cottage

Run by seven generations of Morans, this gorgeous thatched-roof pub has been specializing in Galway Bay seafood since 1966. If you are a seafood lover, do not miss this place. In warm weather, be sure to grab a table outside, so you can enjoy the river views.

http://www.moransoystercottage.com

Liscannor

Vaughan's Anchor Inn

Well-regarded seafood restaurant with an award-winning chef. Friendly and dedicated staff. It's incredible to find such an authentic, excellent place just a few minutes' drive from the Cliffs of Moher, we can't recommend this place highly enough. Do yourself a favor and book a room here.

http://www.vaughans.ie

New Quay

Linane's Lobster Bar

Excellent seafood restaurant with tables looking out on to the docks, where you can watch the fishermen bringing in their catch of the day, soon to end up on your plate. Open every day in summer; check website for hours in off- and shoulder-seasons.

http://linnanesbar.com/

Lisdoonvarna

Roadside Tavern

Laid-back gastropub, in the same family since 1893. The brew their own beer here and you can smell the hops from blocks away. Best burger we've had in all Ireland. Roadside is also well known for its music scene; there is live traditional music every night during the summer season.

http://www.roadsidetavern.ie/roadside/

Adare

The Village Inn

Clean, comfy rooms above Sean Collins' bar. Tea service in the rooms, and a communal fridge in the hallway.

Doubles from 58€.

http://www.seancollinsbaradare.com

Liscannor

Vaughan's Anchor Inn (see listing in Where to Eat)

Cozy, cute rooms upstairs from the restaurant, from 90€. Best breakfast we've had in Ireland, with many homemade, thoughtful touches. Upon arrival, staff delivers a basket of teabags and homemade chocolate chip cookies. Liscannor is a small village, basically just one street, which is remarkable considering its proximity to the Cliffs of Moher.

http://www.vaughans.ie

Shannon

Carrygerry Country House

It's hard to believe this beautiful house, surrounded by fields filled with horses, is just 10 minutes from Shannon's airport. The ground floor boasts an excellent award-winning restaurant; the upper floors have comfortable, well-appointed rooms. If you are flying out of Shannon this is a perfect place to stay for those looking for excellent food and wishing to avoid the cookie-cutter airport hotel experience. Reservations for dinner are necessary.

Double rooms from 75€.

http://www.carrygerryhouse.com

Ennis

Glenomra House B&B

Homey little B&B just 15 minutes from Shannon's airport. It's a 10 minute walk to Ennis town center, where you can find pubs and restaurants. There are a few fast food restaurant options within 3 minutes walk of the B&B.

Double rooms from 70€.

https://www.glenomrahouse.com

Loop Head

Lighthouse

The drive out to Loop Head lighthouse is absolutely stunning, so be sure to give yourself time to take it in. Huge, towering cliffs over azure colored water. When we rent a lighthouse we offset the cost by shopping farm shops and cooking for ourselves. Lighthouses are a bit of a splurge but the scenery is unforgettable.

From 205€/night.

http://www.irishlandmark.com/

Doolin

Twin Peaks B&B

This cozy B&B is in a residential area, just a few minutes' walk from Doolin's pubs and shops. Owners Sinead and Pascal are welcoming and kind hosts, who will cook you a full Irish breakfast to order. There is a large communal room with TV, movies, and open fire guests can share.

Doubles from 80€.

http://www.twinpeaksdoolin.com/

Lisdoonvarna

Royal Spa Hotel

Historic hotel open since 1832 in the cute town of Lisdoonvarna. There is a restaurant and bar downstairs, bar has a cozy atmosphere and open log fires.

Rooms are cozy and comfortable. Note: the Lisdoonvarna Matchmaking Festival runs from the last week of August to the first week of October.

Doubles from 75€.

https://www.royalspahotel.com/

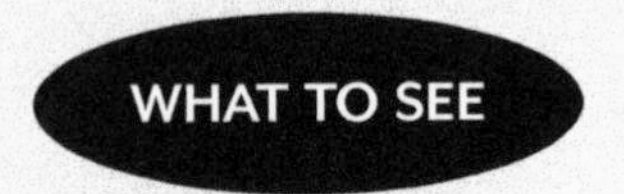

Sights are free to enter unless otherwise noted.

Quin Abbey, St. Bridget's Well (Liscannor), Loop Head Drive, Carrigaholt Castle, Burren National Park, Poulnabrone Dolmen, Corcomroe Abbey, Kilmacduagh Monastery.

Note: At Kilmacduagh, for a 5€ deposit you can borrow the key to the castle and the gates of some of the ruins; inquire at the keeper's house across the street. Yes, really.

Doolin

Clare Jam Company

One mile south of Doolin on the coast road you'll find this small jam shop, where you can purchase homemade jams and mustards, oftentimes made with local ingredients sourced nearby and on the Burren.

https://www.facebook.com/The-Clare-Jam-Company-638087912938304/

Lisdoonvarna

The Burren Smokehouse

Hours vary by season, check website: https://www.burrensmokehouse.com/

Burren Perfumery

A small, family-run shop making soaps, cosmetics, and candles on site, using ingredients sourced from the Burren itself. All natural, organic, and high quality. A lovely little cafe and tea room on site. Extensive and beautiful gardens here you can visit as well. No bus tours allowed, so it maintains a peaceful and calm atmosphere.

Hours vary by season, check website: https://burrenperfumery.com/

ROUTE #3

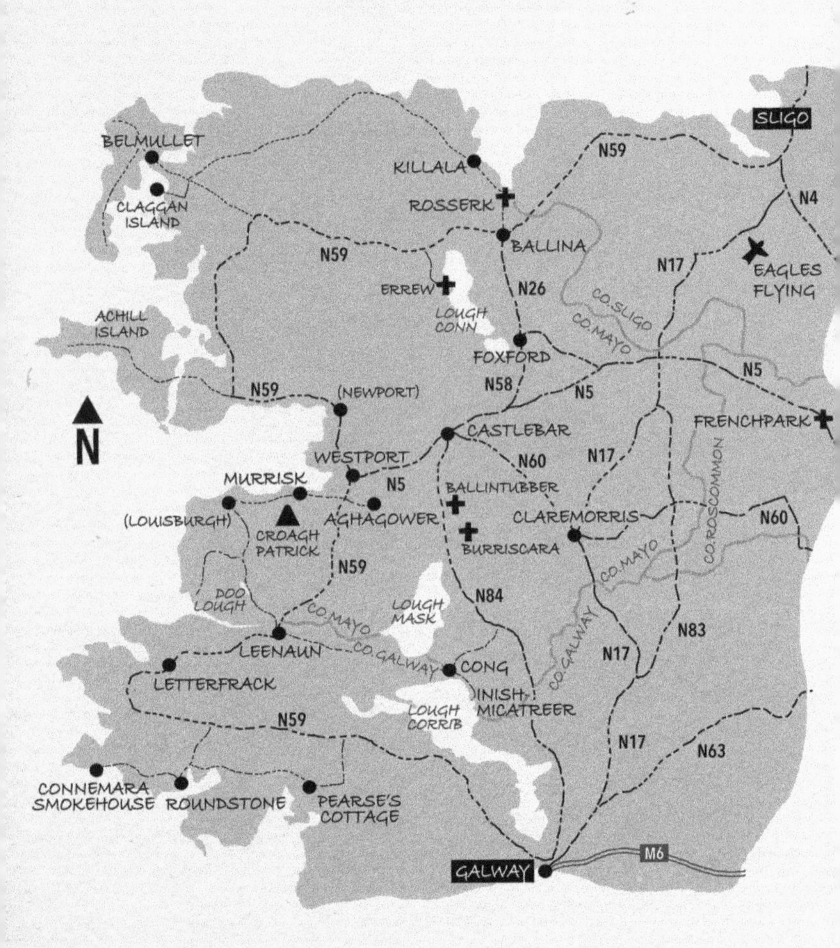

SLIGO
BELMULLET
KILLALA
N59
CLAGGAN ISLAND
ROSSERK
N4
BALLINA
N59
N17
EAGLES FLYING
ERREW
N26
LOUGH CONN
CO. SLIGO
CO. MAYO
ACHILL ISLAND
FOXFORD
N5
N58
N5
N59
(NEWPORT)
FRENCHPARK
CASTLEBAR
WESTPORT
N60
N17
MURRISK
N5
BALLINTUBBER
CO. ROSCOMMON
(LOUISBURGH)
AGHAGOWER
CLAREMORRIS
N60
CROAGH PATRICK
BURRISCARA
N59
CO. MAYO
DOO LOUGH
LOUGH MASK
N84
CO. MAYO
CO. GALWAY
N83
LEENAUN
CO. GALWAY
N17
CONG
LETTERFRACK
INISH MICATREER
LOUGH CORRIB
N59
N17
N63
CONNEMARA SMOKEHOUSE
ROUNDSTONE
PEARSE'S COTTAGE
M6
GALWAY
N

Western Ireland

Counties Galway, Mayo, Sligo

This itinerary covers a wide swath of western Ireland known as Connacht, one of the four traditional regions of Ireland. It's the home of a famous revolutionary and the filming location for at least two well-known films. It explores the coastal counties of Galway, Mayo, and Sligo. Though English is widely spoken here, this region contains some of the thickest concentrations of Irish Gaelic speakers in the country, giving the whole area an extra dash of magic.

Driving west from Galway town, following the Wild Atlantic Way, you'll quickly find yourself in the expansive and beautiful Connemara region, which is sparsely populated and dotted with countless lakes, streams, and sea inlets. John Wayne fans will want to stop at the Quiet Man bridge, the site of a famous scene from the eponymous 1952 film. History buffs should look for signs pointing to **Pearse's Cottage**. This is the humble but evocative thatched home of Patrick Pearse, a hero of the Irish Republic. This recently opened site includes a thoughtfully laid-out museum, and the guide staff are friendly and excited to share their history and heritage.

Patrick Pearse and Irish Independence

The year 1916 is widely regarded as the beginning of the movement to Irish independence from the U.K. A proud Irishman, Patrick Pearse was a teacher, lawyer, poet, and proponent of maintaining the Irish language. He later became one of the "founding fathers" of the Republic of Ireland when in 1916 he became spokesman for the Irish Republican Brotherhood, boldly reading his Proclamation of the Irish Republic, which signaled the Easter Uprising. He and over a dozen comrades were arrested by British authorities and executed, and the initial uprising was quelled; but Pearse's influence led to more Irish insurgencies and eventually to Ireland's independence in 1922.

Head west over the hills toward the village of **Roundstone**. This terrain is stark and mountainous despite the proximity of the coast, more reminiscent of Montana than Ireland. Roundstone, a coastal fishing port, has become something of an artists' colony, and thus has several galleries and a craft centre. The latter is located at The Monastery, the site of a 200-year-old Franciscan settlement of which only a tower remains. Here, find Connemara Pottery, a cozy, wood-smokey studio where artists Seamus and Rose craft beautiful mugs, plates, and jewelry.

Just up the street, overlooking the fishermen's harbor, is **O'Dowds Seafood Bar & Restaurant**. Run by the O'Dowds for five generations, it's the oldest family-run pub in Connemara. Today it's an award-winning gastropub.

O'Dowd's makes a fantastic Guinness beef stew, but their main focus is local seafood. They're known for its creative use of a local food oddity, the carrageen variety of Connemara seaweed. Cooking this seaweed yields a wide range of benefits. It is said to help fight off the flu and other infections, no doubt useful to countless fishermen over the centuries. Boiled down, it also serves as an effective and nutritious thickener for soups, and a vegetarian-friendly gelatin for desserts like puddings and panna cotta.

Farther west, almost to the southwest tip of the peninsula, is the famous **Connemara Smokehouse**, where fish (especially salmon) are smoked using ancient methods. In addition to being a perfect source for authentic foodstuffs of the region, this family-run place is also an "Économusée" site, one of a worldwide network of artisan museums that display the life and creative traditions of diverse and remote communities.

Work your way north along the coast to return to the N59 highway, which loops around back to the east toward the Connemara National Park. Here you'll come to **Cloverfox Restaurant** at the little crossroads town of **Letterfrack**. This cozy pub and restaurant specializes in plates with locally sourced ingredients, from cheese and meats (and fish, of course!) to produce and baked goods. There's a craft shop next door that stocks goods from local artisans.

Travelers wishing to splurge a bit on lodging will want to follow the N59 farther east. You'll pass Kylemore Abbey, a beautiful but touristy lakeside attraction. Eventually the road meets the 10-mile-long and extremely deep **Killary Harbor**, flanked on both sides by steep mountain slopes. Geology nerds will marvel that this glacial sea inlet is in fact a *fjord*, one of only three in all of Ireland. Foodies, on the other hand, will be more interested in this as the source of some of the regions best shellfish. Near the source of the harbor is the tiny village of **Leenaun** (or Leenane). The **Sheep and Wool Center** sells wool and knit goods from some of the thousands of local sheep you've seen for days as you drive this area. This town and the surrounding region was the setting for *The Beauty Queen of Leenane* by Irish playwright Martin McDonagh. It was also the location for yet another well-known film: *The Field* (1990). Among the several pubs in town is **Gaynor's Bar**, also known as The Field Bar. The old pub has a cozy fireplace room that displays a plethora of memorabilia from the movie. (The cast included Sean Bean, whose character, as usual—spoiler alert!—didn't survive the plot.)

Just north of the village sits **Stoneacre**, a vacation rental house. Elevated from the water's edge, the huge picture windows of this lovely house look out west over the harbor and the steep hills on the other side, a perfect place to catch sunsets and rainbows. The living room has a wood-burning stove and an assortment of books, making guests feel like masters of the manor. The kitchen is well-equipped with an AGA stove, allowing serious food people to make excellent use of the local foodstuffs they find in their travels.

One of the highlights of this area, east of Leenaun, is called **Joyce Country**, as it was the ancestral home of the family of novelist James Joyce. Allow ample time to drive these winding hills. Exploring the roads between Leenaun and the town of **Cong** will reward you with gorgeous views of several lakes and idyllic woodlands. At every bend in the road, you'll want to stop and take what you're sure will be an award-winning photo.

The village of Cong itself may be a bit crowded during spring and summer months, but it's a great off-season stop. Visitors interested in falconry can visit the **Falconry Ireland** center, which holds daily exhibitions of various birds of prey. The center is on the grounds of Ashford Castle, dating from the 13th century and a one-time home of the

Guinness family (yes, *that* Guinness), now an upscale resort hotel complex. The real draw though, is a short walk across the river and through the woods to **Cong Abbey**. On the edge of the village, these well-preserved ruins are part of a self-guided walk through history. The High King of Ireland—an O'Connor, naturally—built the abbey in the 12th century atop the remains of a 7th-century settlement. His son, the last High King, died here. The village of Cong itself has several eateries and coffee shops, as well as another monument to *The Quiet Man* (much of which was filmed here), a statue of "The Duke" himself.

Just outside of Cong (northeast on the R345) is **Glebe Stone Circle**, a smaller example of the megaliths of prehistoric Ireland. More of a curiosity than a great marvel, this site actually has four stone circles and other stone structures within a few hundred yards of one another. It's fun to find them all and wonder at the tremendous work that it took for supposedly "primitive" Neolithic men to create these stone formations, and ponder what might have motivated them to do so.

A bit to the south is the large, sprawling Lough Corrib, and an oddity of little note that we like to mention: **Inishmicatreer**. An island in the lake that's accessible by a narrow causeway, it has maybe a dozen homesteads and a couple of small farms, and no commercial area at all. From the causeway, you'll see strange and unexplained stone cairns on a few tiny islands just off the shore, as if they've been there for decades if not for centuries. It's worth a detour for its natural beauty alone. The light playing on the water makes the lake surface a perfect mirror, and this is a beautiful place to watch birds or just take in the solitude and silence.

Returning to Killary Harbor, follow the R335 into County Mayo, west along the fjord and then north toward Louisburgh. This stretch of road, past Doo Lough and over the **Doolough Pass**, is called the Famine Walk. This was the site of one of the more tragic episodes of the 19th-century Irish potato famine: In 1849, starving residents of Louisburgh were directed by British authorities to report to a lodge in the countryside if they wanted rations. Many made the arduous 12-mile walk, only to be refused by the officials there. The return walk was fatal to many of the people, who succumbed to exposure and malnutrition. An inscribed stone cross on the roadside memorializes this tragedy, a particularly shameful example of bureaucracy and indifference to human suffering.

Irish Potato Famine

In 1845, a potato blight swept the island of Ireland, and this plant-sickness persisted for several years, causing the crop of potatoes to wither and fail. In Scotland and parts of mainland Europe this was a problem as well; but because the potato was so singularly vital to the diet of the Irish masses, the resulting starvation among the poorer classes was extreme. The upper classes, and especially the British ruling class, were amply provisioned, but alas the wealth of food seemed not trickle down to those who needed it most. Due to death by malnourishment and subsequent disease, and also due to mass exodus (to, among other places, the U.S.), the island had lost nearly a quarter of its population by 1850. Travelers will come across memorials to these events in nearly every town, large or small; the Great Famine or Great Hunger looms large in Irish history and the Irish psyche.

For those looking for an extremely off-the-beaten-track location, go west to the village of Kil-ladoon. From here, follow signs south to the **Uggool Valley**, also known as The Lost Valley. These are tiny roads, often with room for just one car. The road cuts across miles of farmland to a small parking lot and a huge beachhead. This is the Silver Strand. At low tide it's a half-mile walk to the water across a wide swath of rippled sand. There's nothing to be found here but the solitude. It's actually the farmstead of a centuries-old family that has only in recent decades made the land accessible to public visitors.

Continuing on the road towards Westport, you'll see the looming peak of **Croagh Patrick** to the south. This is probably the most important Catholic pilgrimage site in all of Ireland. The fabled Saint Patrick is said to have climbed this 2500-foot mountain and fasted for 40 days, after which he descended and drove all the snakes out of Ireland. On the last Sunday in July every

year, tens of thousands of pilgrims make the trek up the mountain to show their devotions at its centuries-old oratory. Before Saint Patrick, however, the peak had already been a sacred pagan site for thousands of years, which may be why it was adopted into Christian folklore.

The town of **Murrisk**, at the foot of Croagh Patrick, is a visitor center and a base for walks up the peak. In the town park is a memorial: A grim metal ship festooned with skeletons, representing the "coffin ships" that carried ill-fated Irish people in their attempts to escape the ravaging conditions of the famine. Less grim but equally thought-provoking are the nearby remains of **Murrisk Abbey**, dating from the 15th century and said to have been built on the site of a church that Patrick founded here.

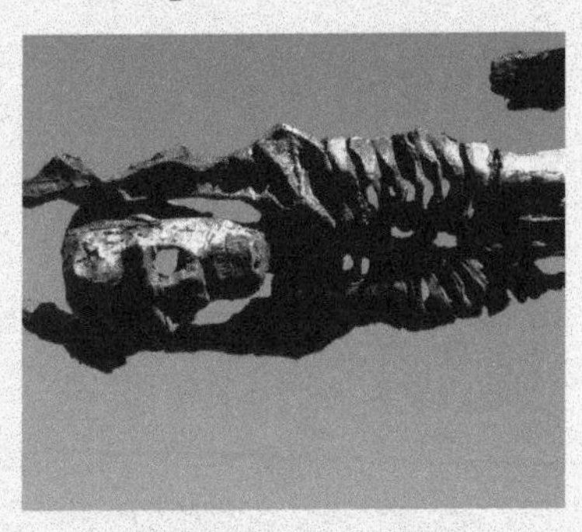

Down the road from the abbey is a nice eatery, the **Tavern Bar and Restaurant**. Undoubtedly busy during "pilgrimage season", this charming place is quiet in the off-months. The highlight here is a brown-bread ice cream, inspired by and made with the iconic Irish soda bread that accompanies every meal in Ireland.

Just a bit to the south and east is **Aghagower**, a tiny village with seemingly more dead people than living. The town is on the path that Patrick took on his long walk up to the mountain, so for centuries many residents of the area have seen to it to that they be buried here on the hallowed ground near the town's medieval church ruin, round tower, and holy well.

Driving north you'll come at last to the bustling town of **Westport**, famous for live traditional music and confusing traffic patterns. Count on taking at least one unintentional drive through the town. Just stay calm and go with the traffic flow! Eventually you'll sort it out and find

your way to its many fine establishments: **Matt Molloy's**, a pub owned by the flute player of famous Irish band The Chieftains, has live music nightly. Many such pubs here don't offer food, but there's plenty to be had. Check out the fare at the **Cobbler's Bar**, the pub connected to the **Wyatt Hotel**. This is one of two lodgings we recommend in Westport. The other is an old historic family-run lodge, the B&B at **McCarthy's Bar**.

The town is a great place to do an extensive pub crawl, and you can stroll along its picturesque riverside street that follows the Carrowbeg River. The bridge crossings are usually decorated with flowers and other decorations connected to the

many festivals that go on year-round. You name the interest, Westport has a festival for it: chamber music, modern art, food, fishing, crafts, poker, hot rods, driftwood (yes, you read that right), and, of course, traditional Irish music.

A short trip east along the N5 is **Castlebar**, a fair-sized crossroads town notable for an excellent food stop. **Rua Café and Delicatessen** stocks high-end local foodstuffs and offers a wide array of prepared dishes. We've been known to drive miles out of our way to stop here in order to deplete their supply of Llewellen's apple syrup and apple balsamic vinegar, an Irish product that we love. The shop is across the street from "The Mall", a green square that sports a fascinating bronze sculpture depicting legendary hero Manannan Mac Lir and his horse springing from the sea. A coffee or tea from Rua to take away makes for a lovely little stroll around the neighborhood.

To the south on the N84 are two ancient and historic sites, the 13th-century abbeys of **Burriscarra** and **Ballintubber**. The former is a lonely ruin. The latter is now the site of a restored and active church, so be respectful of the locals when you visit this ancient place. There is a holy well on the grounds that St Patrick is said to have consecrated in the 5th century. It is from this site that he is said to have set out on his journey west to climb Croagh Patrick.

Farther east along tiny roads (or southeast from Castlebar on the N60) is another food town, **Claremorris**. Here you should sate your appetite for biscuits and scones at **Aghna's Coffee Bar**, which prepares soups and sandwiches as well, and all to a high level of quality. Have a hearty breakfast or lunch here, then stroll over to get your groceries at the adjacent and imaginatively named **Food Store**, another combination grocery and deli with a full butchery and bakery.

Continuing north from Westport on the N59, pass through the bridge town of Newport and find signs to **Burrishoole Abbey**. This waterside 15th-century Dominican friary is a picturesque ruin. A few of the buildings have intact windows and carvings. On a clear day, one can look south across Clew Bay to the peak of Croagh Patrick.

Follow the N59 farther west until it turns north away from the bay, and look for the little R319 highway. This road winds north and west until it crosses a bridge onto **Achill Island**, Ireland's largest island. Right before the bridge is a "Óstán Oileán Acla" (Achill Island Hotel) with a lovely pub/restaurant, **Alice's Bar**. This is a fine place for a seafood lunch with wide views over the sound.

Achill Island is an idyllic retreat for artists and surfers, as well as history buffs: sand beaches and white cliffs, ancient church ruins and an aban-

doned famine village, a 15th-century seaside castle tower that belonged to the infamous "Pirate Queen" Grace O'Malley. Achill is remote and wild, with every turn in its roads providing a new and beautiful coastal view or historical marker.

Again returning to the N59, continue north to the village of Bangor Erris. It's worth a few minutes to follow the N59 through town to the east, where you'll soon come to a bronze statue on the roadside that remembers the Famine Years: This is a nod to the parting of ways that many families were compelled to take during this time. A mother and child are waving goodbye to departing loved ones, in many cases never to be seen again.

From Bangor Erris, take the R313 west to another coastal section, the **Belmullet Peninsula** on Blacksod Bay. The peninsula has a few villages (including working fishing towns, naturally), several lighthouses, and no shortage of views. An excellent lodging from which to explore this area is across the bay at the **Claggan Island Coast Guard Station**, a restored maritime facility (originally built in 1795) that's now the fourth-generation farmstead of the Howard family. This self-catering apartment is modern, clean, and comfortable, with a turf-burning stove for heat. The Howards are directly next door if guests need help. They also offer less expensive "luxury pods"—little self-contained wooden cabins out on the lawn overlooking the bay. Either way, this little pocket of Ireland is remote. "City folks" will marvel at the abundance of stars in the sky at night... and the large number of chickens greeting them on the lawn in the morning.

Claggan isn't exactly an island. It is connected to the mainland by a "causeway", a narrow path between two sand-dune ridges in the bay, surrounded by water in both directions. A stay out here is not just gorgeous and remote; driving this stretch of beach to the station feels like you're venturing onto the secret retreat of some eccentric and reclusive author or former world leader.

Just outside the lodging is a historical site and a modern art installation: "Acknowledgement" speaks to an ugly aspect of the Famine Years: Many children died before they were old enough to be baptized. The church determined that because they were not baptized, they were not eligible for a Christian burial. So this is the site of one of the unconsecrated mass graves for child victims of the famine. The memorial on the sculpture heartbreakingly reads:

"They are begging us, you see, in their wordless way.
To do something, to speak on their behalf
Or at least not to close the door again"

This is just one of a series of a dozen or so works on the **Tír Sáile,** a.k.a. the **North Mayo Sculpture Trail**. A few others are on Belmullet Peninsula, and many are off the highway that crawls along the northern coast of County Mayo.

This highway is the R314. It leads past a handful of quaint little villages and many acres of pastureland and colorful hillsides to the Ceide Fields archaeological site. Here the pyramidal visitor's center is a gateway to the remains of a Neolithic farming settlement. Dating from before 3000 BC, it's the oldest known field system in the world. This site overlooks the North Atlantic from atop some sheer and impressive stratified cliffs.

Farther east, past the town of Ballycastle, you'll come to the cute village of **Killala**, at the top of which is a medieval round tower. This is evidently another haven for at least one artist: Next to the tower we found a mural representing the town itself, and elsewhere in the town can be found other murals depicting historical figures of the town.

To the south of Killala are several ancient monastery sites. Along the west bank of the River Moy is **Moyne Abbey**, and further south is **Rosserk Friary**. The latter is remarkable in that it has an intact second floor, which originally held the monks' lodgings and kitchen. Two fireplaces and a lot of other carved and crafted stonework are

still well preserved despite the centuries. Both of these abbeys escaped destruction by the "suppression" of Henry VIII... only to be destroyed by one of the agents of Elizabeth I a few decades later.

These wanderings down the Moy River lead eventually to the town of **Ballina**. A few minutes up the road directly on the other side of the river, you'll find **Crocketts on the Quay**. Well-known throughout the country for its high-quality and elegant food offerings, this gastropub is beautiful—all brass rails and polished wood beams and artistic mirrors.

About 15 minutes to the south, toward Lough Conn, is the home of **Foxford Woolen Mills**. The mill was founded in Foxford by the Convent of the Divine Providence in 1892, one of many efforts to revitalize blighted towns and regions after the Famine Years. Today the town is a center for commerce, and the mills still produce fine wool products. A scarf or sweater from here is a useful and unique souvenir of your visit to County Mayo.

Foxford is on the east side of Lough Conn. On a peninsula on the west side of the lake, for the truly dogged explorers, is another medieval site, **Errew Abbey**. It can be reached after a series of this-can't-still-be-right turns down tiny roads, and then a short walk through woods and a cow field. You're rewarded with a visit to a 12th-century monastic outpost built on the remains of an even older (6th century) settlement. Though there are many such historical sites in Mayo (and throughout Ireland), there are few that offer this kind of remoteness. The fact that such places were established in such far-flung locations speaks volumes of that devotion of the men and women who built these places.

This devotion took many forms, including care of the dead, as evidenced by the well-kept cemeteries at all of these historic sites. A remarkable example of that is at **Cloonshanville Abbey**, in Frenchpark on the N5 (east from Foxford, just into County Roscommon). The remains of this 14th-century monastic settlement are more ruinous than normal. The shell of the tower is eerily covered in ivy. Near the monastery stand the remains of a high cross. Legend has it that villagers would carry their dead to the cross, and the monks would collect the bodies for preparation and burial. Unusually, the site includes a more-or-less intact mausoleum—of the family French, after whom the village is named—with much intricate stonework, including a stone-carved crucifix.

Driving north into County Sligo, you may visit a place devoted to the natural rather than the supernatural: the **Eagles Flying** wildlife refuge. Daily bird shows—including, you guessed it, eagles flying—teach audiences not just about these fascinating birds, but also about ecology and conservation, about balance in nature, and about the role of humans in all of these aspects of the natural world. (Hint: It's not always positive.) Originally a research center specializing in raptor birds, the facility is now a haven for injured and otherwise at-risk animals of all kinds—nearly 400 animals in some 75 species—from around the countryside.

Making your way north to the N4 will bring you at last to Sligo town. This is a large town (by "Little Roads" standards at least), historic and bustling, with a wide array of restaurants, pubs, and lodgings. An impressive cathedral overlooks the town. It's modern by Irish reckoning, at only about 150 years old.

About the same age is our favorite eatery here,

Hargadon Brothers, just a few blocks away in the commercial district. Formerly a grocers and spirit shop, Hargadon's is now a gastropub with no end of charm. They serve fresh food of the highest quality, organic and locally sourced whenever possible. The chefs are personally connected to the farmers, the fishermen, the butchers and the vintners, who supply their kitchen and their cellar. Even in a town as big as this is, you can still escape, if you know where to go. Here you can step back a century or two into cozy, perfectly preserved, wood-paneled rooms sporting original fixtures and vintage furniture. Whether stopping in for a pint, or joining the old ladies for a tea service, or tucking in to a hearty lunch or dinner, Hargadon's is the perfect blend of the historic and the modern.

Restaurants are open every day for lunch and dinner unless otherwise noted.

Roundstone

O'Dowds Seafood Bar and Restaurant

Excellent gastro pub in an idyllic seaside town, using locally sourced ingredients, including many from their own gardens. The pub uses seafood in a remarkable variety of dishes, including dessert. Reservations recommended.

http://www.odowdsseafoodbar.com/

Letterfrack

Clover Fox Restaurant

Upscale restaurant with a cozy environment, serving the highest quality locally sourced ingredients. Extensive wine list and craft beers on tap. Next door there is a shop featuring work of local artisans. Reservations recommended.

http://cloverfox.ie/

Sligo

Hargadon Brothers

In days past this pub was a pub and grocer's, today it is a well regarded gastropub. Well worth the trip here just for the food, but a bonus is the incredible interior, which is like taking a step back in time. Open for lunch and dinner Monday - Saturday, bar only Sunday nights.

http://www.hargadons.com/

Murrisk

The Tavern

Extensive menu, beautifully presented, with many items featuring locally sourced products. Be sure to try the brown bread ice cream. Great local beer offerings.

http://www.tavernmurrisk.com

Ballina

Crockett's on the Quay

Locally popular pub, beautiful interiors and generous portions. Reservations recommended, especially for Sunday lunch.

http://www.crocketsonthequay.ie/

Claremorris

Aghna's Coffee Bar

Little cafe where you can find fresh baked goods, a hot breakfast or lunch, soups, sandwiches, salads, much of it made on the premises. Also has a little shop selling local cheese, meat, and produce. A perfect place to stop for a cappuccino and a slice of cake.

Open Monday - Saturday 9 - 5:30, closed Sunday. On Dalton Street in Claremorris.

Leenaun

Stonacre

Absolutely gorgeous home located at the tip of Killary Harbour. The house sits up on a little hill, which commands stunning views of the bay, from the home's large picture windows, and also its gardens. As this is a home, it has all the amenities one could want, including a working fireplace.

From 135€/night.

https://www.holidaylettings.co.uk/rentals/leenane/87473

Westport

The Wyatt Hotel

Boutique hotel in the center of Westport. Comfy beds, free parking and wifi. Restaurant and bar downstairs, room service is available.

Doubles from 48€.

http://www.wyatthotel.com

McCarthy's Lodge & Bar

This family-owned pub has several rooms upstairs, and larger apartments for rent as well. Full Irish breakfast on offer in the morning.

Doubles from 80€.

http://www.mccarthyslodge.com/

Claggan Island

Belmullet Coast Guard Station

Formerly the Coast Guard Station on remote Claggan Island, today a special vacation rental. To get to the island you drive on a long sandbar, which is an experience in itself. Home to a family who also lives at the station, they are available if you need them but respect your privacy. The house you rent out is private, with a large kitchen, two bedrooms, and an upstairs den with working fireplace. The stars at night are incredible, as are the views during the day.

Minimum stay 2 nights, from 250€ for 2 nights, discounts for longer stays.

http://belmulletcgs.com/

Sights are free to enter unless otherwise noted.

Pearse's Cottage, Joyce Country (drive), Cong Abbey, Glebe stone circle, Inishmicatreer island, Doolough Pass, Uggool Valley, Croagh Patrick, Murrisk Abbey, Aghagower town, Burriscarra Abbey, Ballintubber Abbey, Burrishoole Abbey, Achill Island, North Mayo Sculpture Trail, Moyne Abbey, Rosserk Friary, Errew Abbey, Cloonshanville Abbey.

Claremorris

The Food Store

Lovely little family-run shop with a butchery, bakery, and deli. A great place to stock up on local artisan foods like cheese, honey, and jams, or to find well-made prepared foods to eat at home. Open every day until 6pm.

https://www.thefoodstore.ie/

Castlebar

Cafe Rua

Also a cafe, which is mobbed by locals every day. This place is so successful it is able to sustain two cafes in the small town. The Spencer Street location holds the shop, which is a gold mine of Irish artisan foods. We stop here to pick up Christmas gifts for everyone on our list. Be sure to try the apple syrup and apple cider balsamic vinegar, both made by Llewellyn's Farm. Closed Sunday.

http://www.caferua.com/

Roundstone

Roundstone Ceramics

Rosemarie and Seamus run this beautiful little ceramics shop, you can watch them work as you shop. Rosemarie makes ceramic jewelry as well. In addition to being great artists, they are friendly people. Open every day from 10-6 from April-October. For store hours from November-March, call the shop at 09535874.

Foxford

Foxford Woolen Mill

They've been weaving wool here on site since 1892, and is an integral part of the local community. Today it's a large, modern mill and shop (you can watch the wool being woven from the shop), and there is a nice cafe here as well.

Open Monday - Saturday 10-6, Sunday 12-6.

https://www.foxfordwoollenmills.com/

ROUTE #4

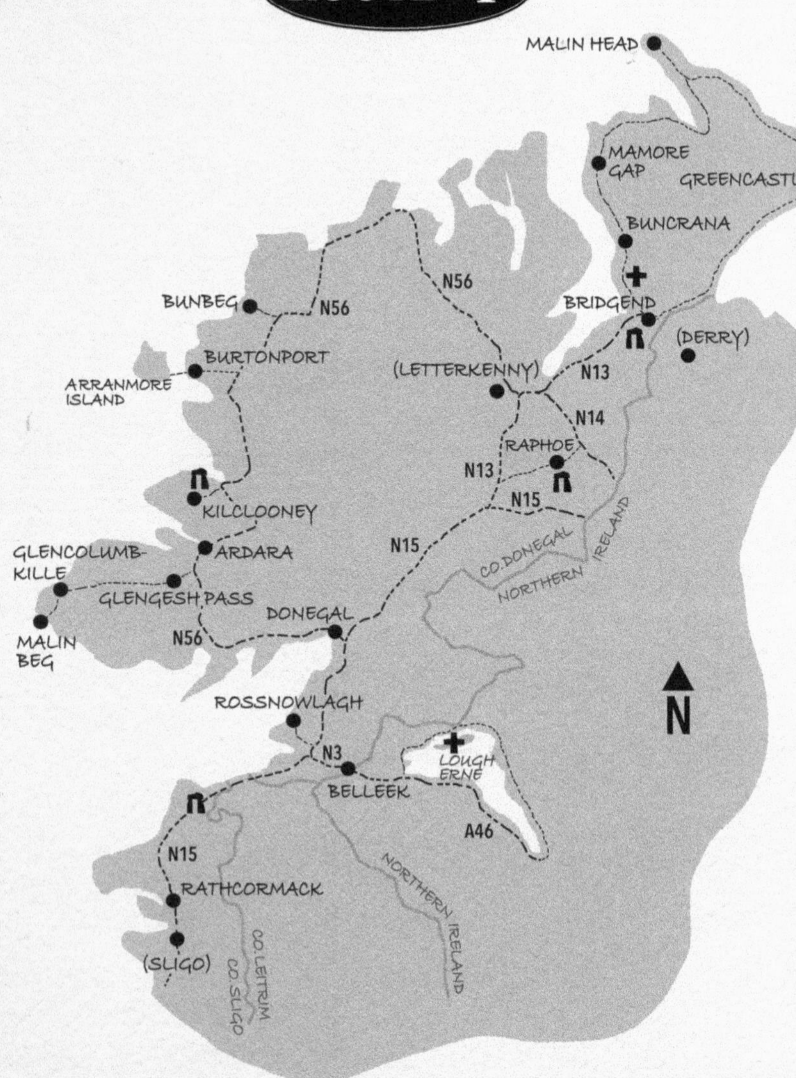

MALIN HEAD
MAMORE GAP
GREENCASTL
BUNCRANA
N56
BUNBEG
N56
BRIDGEND
(DERRY)
BURTONPORT
ARRANMORE ISLAND
(LETTERKENNY)
N13
N14
RAPHOE
N13
N15
KILCLOONEY
N15
ARDARA
GLENCOLUMB-KILLE
GLENGESH PASS
CO.DONEGAL
NORTHERN IRELAND
DONEGAL
MALIN BEG
N56
ROSSNOWLAGH
N
N3
LOUGH ERNE
BELLEEK
A46
N15
RATHCORMACK
NORTHERN IRELAND
CO. LEITRIM
CO. SLIGO
(SLIGO)

Northwest Ireland

Co. Donegal and Vicinity

County Donegal dominates the northwest of Ireland. It's the fourth largest, least-populated, and northernmost county in Ireland. Donegal is a land of sweeping green mountain valleys dotted with countless sheep, sheer seaside cliffs descending to jagged rocky coastline or beautiful white-sand beaches, and excellent food to be had throughout—if you know where to look.

Driving north up the N15 highway from Sligo, stop at the little roadside **Vintage Lane Café** in Rathcormack. Tucked in among several antique shops and craft stores, this little family-run coffee shop serves some of the best coffee we've had in Ireland, as well as delicious homemade baked goods. Travelers with a literary interest will want to take note of a headstone in a nearby churchyard, the final resting place (probably) of Irish poet W.B. Yeats. The Sligo area was Yeats' ancestral home, and several sites in the area are connected to his life and times.

W. B. Yeats

The famous poet W. B. Yeats spent many a summer in or around Sligo, as a child and in adulthood. He drew a lot of inspiration from the landscape of the region, naming many local places in his poetry. Though he died in France in 1939, his body was shipped to Sligo nine years later and buried in Drumcliffe north of Sligo town—though some controversy lurks suggesting they actually sent the wrong cadaver.

After slaking your thirst for poetry (or caffeine), continue north on the N15. You'll soon find the roadside marker for **Creevykeel tomb**, right off the highway. This is a fine example of a Neolithic stone structure, this one a 5000-year-old "court cairn" (a burial chamber surrounded by a larger "room" delineated by a wall made from large stones). It's also a great example of how so many of these ancient sites of prehistory are easy and free to visit.

Upon entering County Donegal itself, divert from the main highway to follow signs to **Rossnowlagh** and its 1.5-mile stretch of smooth beach surrounded by cliffs. This beach is special. Cars are permitted to drive on it, and at low tide it is a gorgeous, firm-sand parking area for surfers, beachgoers, and picnickers. Perched on top of the cliff overlooking the beach is the **Smugglers Creek Inn**, where you can treat yourself to a pint and a steaming bowl of seafood chowder on the patio.

From here, the sweeping view of the landscape—the beach, the peninsula, the bay leading out to the ocean beyond—gives the impression that you're seeing the whole world below.

If you're carrying a few extra pounds—British pounds, that is—you may consider a quick excursion east into Northern Ireland, which here extends nearly to the west coast of Ireland. Just over the border on the River Erne is the town of **Belleek**. The town is famous for its pottery center (or *centre* as they call it here). Stop in at the **Black Cat Cove**, a neighborhood gastropub known for its locally sourced plates and perfectly pulled pints. The Black Cat is a popular evening hangout as well, as it hosts live musicians every night in spring and summer.

Follow the River Erne east until it opens up into a lake, **Lower Lough Erne**. A few hours' drive

Ireland's Four Historical Provinces

Visitors to Ireland quickly become familiar with its county divisions—County Cork, County Clare, and so on, 32 in total. But these are relatively recent divisions. A thousand years ago or so, four broadly defined "kingdoms" were established: Leinster in the east; Munster in the southwest; Connacht in the west; and Ulster in the north, which included Donegal. A high king would have ruled over all of these, with lower level rulers in each kingdom. Each contained sub-regions now known as counties. Some confusion lies with Ulster, which is sometimes used interchangeably (and incorrectly) to refer to Northern Ireland; in fact, six out of nine counties of Ulster remained in the U.K. in the 1900s when the rest of Ireland split to become its own nation.

around the lake is rewarded with many highlights, from castles to tombstones to parks. On the south shore is **Tully Castle**, a ruined fortification from the 17th century. It sits on a walking trail that circumnavigates the lake. A walk around the grounds is free, and it's a perfect place for a picnic overlooking the lake.

On the north side of the lake is a narrow island strip called **Boa Island**, which has a causeway running its length. It is sparsely populated, but one fascinating stop is the little **Caldragh Cemetery** in more or less the exact center of the island. The graveyard includes two carved stone figures dating from early Christian times. One has two faces like the Roman god Janus, while the other seems to have only one completely carved eye, suggesting the legendary Caillech Bhéarra, the "Crone" figure of Celtic mythology (from which the name Boa probably comes). Though these date from early Christian times, that then-obscure cult had perhaps not yet spread to these remote reaches, hence the pagan nature of the figures.

Returning to the coast and proceeding north, we come to County Donegal's namesake, a town on the River Eske that's been an important commerce point for millennia. **Donegal town** has a small but bustling commercial center and a 500-year-old medieval fortification, Donegal Castle, that offers an inexpensive but fascinating foray into Irish history. In medieval times the castle belonged to the famous and powerful O'Donnell clan, which for centuries controlled much of this region of Ireland. Next door to the castle is the picturesque **Olde Castle Bar**, a favorite for tourists due to its proximity, but offering dishes made with locally sourced seafood and meats.

Driving west from Donegal, continue along the coast, where views alternate incongruously between rocky ocean shoreline and green rolling hills; between fishing towns and sheep farms. This is the route to the Slieve League cliffs, which plunge nearly 2000 feet to the ocean below. These cliffs are among the highest in Europe, double the height of those of Moher in County Clare. Farther out on this peninsula is **Malin Beg**, where intrepid hikers can walk cliff pathways, and the beautiful Silver Sand beach.

Heading north around this peninsula leads to the **Glencolmcille Folk Village**, a series of authentically thatched buildings and several museum displays. Here, get a feel for what life was like in this wild and rugged country in past centuries. A short drive southeast into the valley is the **Glencolmcille Woollen Mill** factory shop, where fine wool goods are sold. This is, of course, the main reason all those countless thousands of sheep dot the landscape here.

Between Malin Beg and Glencolmcille are several megaliths. As usual, look for the brown signs, especially the one to the **Malin More** site (off the R263), where six prehistoric tombs are lined up in a row. Or, easier still, just down the road (southeast) from the wool shop is a tiny parking area on the right. Follow the pathway a scant 50 yards to the **Cloghanmore** site, a Neolithic stone formation in the shape of a "court tomb", a burial chamber surrounded by a walled courtyard.

Meandering north and east, we find our way back to the N56 road by way of the breathtaking **Glengesh Pass**, and head into the busy little town of **Ardara**. Here amongst the shops and pubs we find historic **Nancy's Bar**, a local favorite that's been run by the same family for seven generations. The place is a museum of local history as well as a gastropub serving up delicious traditional plates. Be sure to take a peek into all of the rooms. Being in Nancy's is like stepping into an adult-sized doll-house, with each room decorated with artifacts of town life through the decades and centuries.

Leave the highway (such as it is) to follow the smaller R261, which keeps closer to the coastal inlets. Before long, you'll come to Kilclooney and the Dolmen Center. From this community center it's just a 10-minute walk through farmers' fields to the 5000-year-old **Kilclooney Dolmen**. This is a beautiful example of a Neolithic portal tomb. Its heavy capstone is balanced atop several smaller stones, creating an open-ended, roofed chamber. The surrounding hillside is remote, peaceful, magical. It's easy to see why the ancients chose such a location to honor their spirituality, and to memorialize their dead.

Continuing along the road brings you back around to the N56. There's a great deal of coastline to explore here, but for now we press on to the little fishing village of **Burtonport**. Just a block from the docks is the locally famous **Lobster Pot** restaurant. Ask your bartender what's fresh that day, as you're just steps away from where the fishermen drop off their daily catch.

The docks include the boarding area for he ferry to nearby **Arranmore Island**. The cost of the round-trip ferry ride with a car is around $45, and it's much cheaper for walkers or cyclists. There are a couple of pubs on the island, but a better bet might be an inexpensive picnic lunch to enjoy in one of many well-placed picnic

tables around the island. The 15-minute ferry ride itself is fascinating. The boat threads its way amongst a handful of tiny, rocky islands, so narrow that from a distance the naked eye can't make out a passage at all. This is a mystical and beautiful island largely untouched by tourists—a lovely place for hiking, biking, or a leisurely drive out to its remote (and still working) lighthouse, as long as you don't mind sharing the road with the occasional stray sheep.

Arranmore, settled since prehistoric times, is just a few miles from the coast of Ireland. Many of the island's former residents left during the famine years of the 19th century and emigrated to the U.S., where they settled on Beaver Island in the middle of Lake Michigan. To this day, many residents of Beaver Island trace their ancestry to Arranmore, and the two islands are now "twinned" with one another. A monument to this connection stands in a little lake on the island, flying the two countries' flags over statues of an otter, a beaver, and a fish symbolizing the link between the two.

Winding your way farther north along the coast, you'll come to another picturesque fishing village, **Bunbeg.** ("Bun-" is Irish for the mouth of a river on a coast, hence the many coastal town names with this prefix.) Here visitors can catch ferries to a few of the nearby islands, or they can rest at the comfortable **Bunbeg House** lodging, which has a restaurant and offers rooms overlooking the little inlet harbor and quay.

From here, drivers must first venture south (and east) to go still farther north, as you approach the base of the huge Inishowen peninsula region. Inishowen contains the northernmost point of mainland Ireland, but there's a lot to see and do

before getting there. Drivers will encounter countless brown signs marked "Inis Eoghain 100". These denote landmarks along a roughly 100-mile stretch of the Inishowen coast, a local version of the Wild Atlantic Way that winds over 1500 miles up the entire western coast of Ireland.

A few kilometers south of the little town of Raphoe, look for signs down tiny roads to **Beltany stone circle**. You can park just outside the Potato Propagation Centre—no, really—and walk about a half a kilometer up the path to a meadow atop a broad hill, where sits this Neolithic structure, one of the largest stone circles in Ireland. One of its 64 stones is a peculiar cup-marked obelisk, which lines up with the rising sun on what we now call May Day, but the ancient Irish called *Bealtaine*—giving the megalith's modern name.

Turn north to find the **Grianan of Aileach**, a circular stone hilltop fort dating from around 1700 BC. This was a legendary defensive settlement for various kings and giants for centuries, and it's easy to see why: Visitors can climb the stone steps inside and walk the circumference of the fort, which commands 360-degree views of the countryside. The interior is reminiscent of being in a small colosseum, three stories high, and the exterior is a windy watch-point overlooking the world.

Continuing still farther north, take the N13 road east almost into the U.K.'s Northern Ireland. Here is the unremarkable town of Bridgend (or Bridge End), and its quite remarkable gastropub **Harry's Bar**, which makes a point of using all locally-sourced and seasonal ingredients. In 2012, Harry's instituted a tradition, taking its food-culture ethos one step further: Every Saturday morning, the parking lot is the site of a farmers' market, at which a dozen or more bakers, ranchers, vegetable farmers, dairy producers, and

fishmongers offer their foodstuffs for sale. Harry's is emblematic of Ireland's resurgent local, sustainable, whole-food movement.

After stocking up on high-quality foodstuffs, or just stuffing yourself like livestock at lunch, turn north on the R238 to begin to trace the west coast of the Inishowen peninsula. (There's a route on the east coast of the peninsula with the same number, but this should not cause too much confusion, as most of the time you won't see route numbers on direction signs anyway.) On the way north, stop for a quick look at the **Fahan Mura cross slab** at a 6th-century monastic site. Unlike the decorated Irish high crosses, this type of early Christian artifact resembles a large tombstone, with an elaborate decorated cross figure carved upon it. This one features carvings on both sides, including two standing figures (children? saints? kings?) and birds perched on or flying above the cross. This site will be on your right as you head north, then on your left as you turn around after realizing you just passed it.

Make your way to **Buncrana**, a moderate-sized but walkable coastal town, with many pubs, cafes, and shops. Just north of downtown is **St Bridget's B&B**, a lovely little place that innkeeper Winnie Doherty has been running for decades, providing comfortable rooms and home-cooked breakfasts in a charming sitting room. A stroll out the door and down the street brings walkers and bikers to a long and beautiful strand of public beach and green space. This is Amazing Grace Park, in recognition of John Newton, a slave-trade sailor turned abolitionist, and writer of the famous hymn. His change of heart came after a shipwreck washed him to shore here in Buncrana's Lough Swilly. Picnic benches are well-placed to relax and look out west over the water

(which is not actually a lake but a sea inlet, one of Ireland's three fjords), making this a great place to catch a sunset.

At the other end of the beach is the aptly named **Beach House Bar & Restaurant**. Here, sitting by large picture windows that look out over the beach, diners enjoy traditional dishes in beautiful, modern presentations, sourcing their meats, dairy, and fish (of course!) locally, baking their own bread, growing their own herbs, and churning their own ice cream.

There are vast stretches of winding coastline between Buncrana and the tip of Inishowen, but one spot really catches our attention when we explore the area: **Mamore Gap**, northwest off of the (unnumbered) highway that runs northeast from Dunree Head to Clonmany. This road is worth the detour for its stunningly straight climb up the Urris Hills and its dizzying panorama of the ocean and the mountains; for its holy well near the crest, dedicated to Saint Eigne; and for its curious so-called "Magic Road" or "Gravity Hill", just beyond the crest on the sea-side of the pass. Here, cars left in neutral on the road will seem to roll uphill of their own accord, so park with great care. (We won't tell you the secret to this place—we don't want to spoil the magic!)

In Clonmany, find again the R238 road, and follow that around to R242, which at last heads north to **Malin Head**, Ireland's northernmost point. The rocks at the very tip of the head are called "Banba's Crown", and they have an important history. In 1805 this was a guard post to defend against the French. A hundred years later, after being converted to a transatlantic radio relay point, it once again became a key observation post in both World Wars of the 20th century. Today it is still an important lookout point, but now just for birds and dolphins rather than U-boats. Walking trails explore the cliffs, but much here is inaccessible due to dangerous footing. Stay safe and stick to the paths.

It's a long stretch from Malin Head to the far eastern point of Inishowen peninsula, filled with gorgeous and picturesque landscapes (and seascapes). On the way, look for the **Clonca Church and High Cross** monastic site off the R238. The ruin of the church here dates from the 17th century, but parts of it are much older. On the grounds you'll also find a high Celtic cross with carvings of lions and saints, and a scene depicting the miracle of the loaves and fishes.

Near the northeastern point of Inishowen, you'll find the busy little fishing village of Greencastle. Just north of the town itself is a ruined castle that's now covered in vines and greenery. This is **Norrhburg Castle**, dating from 1305. Though it's in ruins now, it was once a great fortress, built in part out of the living cliff rock. A quick walk through the ruins is creepy, as even in broad daylight the overgrowth makes the place dark and eerie. After all this exploring, travelers can reward themselves for a tough day of sightseeing with a meal at the family-run, award-winning **Kealy's Seafood Bar**. Their seafood chowder is a special recipe that includes green peppercorns and dill, and their Irish brown bread is served in individual scone-shape buns rather than the usual sliced loaf. As Greencastle is the center of much of Inishowen's fishing industry (indeed, it is home to the National Fisheries College as well as the Inishowen Maritime Museum), Kealy's is perfectly

positioned to offer the best and freshest in traditional seafood dishes. Following the R238 south along the waters of Lough Foyle (another sea inlet, not actually a lake) will lead you past many little fishing villages to the town of Derry/Londonderry on the Northern Ireland border.

County Donegal is large, wild, and remote. Locals like to say, "Up here, it's different." And it is. Even in the high tourist season, you can drive for dozens of miles without seeing anyone but sheep. Take the time to explore another coastal bend, another lake or inlet, another winding mountain road. You never know what you'll find.

Restaurants are open every day for lunch and dinner unless otherwise noted.

Belleek

The Black Cat Cove

The Black Cat Cove in the tiny, cute town of Belleek is well worth a stop. It's not much to look at on the outside, doesn't have a polished web presence, and inside it reads like a traditional Irish pub. But they have spent considerable time and effort on the food, which is presented beautifully and of high quality. This is one of those places that the locals know about, everyone told us we had to eat here.

https://www.facebook.com/TheBlackCatCove/

Ardara

Nancy's Bar

Highly regarded gastro pub, in the same family for seven generations. You won't want to miss this one just for the food, but it's worth it to stop here just for the atmosphere. Each room is themed and chock full of local artifacts; be sure to take a walk through each one.

http://www.nancysardara.com

Burtonport

The Lobster Pot

This pub is just steps from the sea, and so the food miles on your seafood are measured in meters, not miles. This is the place to go to try local seafood – their signature dish is "The Titanic", a huge plate of a variety of fish and shellfish. Pub food served all day, but you will want to arrive between 12-2 or after 6pm, when the specials are on offer.

http://lobsterpot.ie/

Buncrana

Beach House Bar & Restaurant

Upscale restaurant with modern decor serving locally sourced, seasonal food. Be sure to book one of the window tables – the views are unbelievable. Friendly service from people who genuinely care about quality.

Closed Monday - Wednesday. Open for dinner Thursday and Friday. Open for lunch and dinner Saturday and Sunday.

http://thebeachhouse.ie/

Greencastle

Kealy's Seafood Bar

Family-run restaurant that specializes in seafood, which is perfect, since the water is just steps away. This pub is famous for its seafood chowder, which unusually features dill, and pink peppercorns. It's served with their equally famous muffin - sized glazed brown bread scones.

http://www.kealysseafoodbar.ie/

Bunbeg

Bunbeg House

Comfortable little guest house situated down by a pier. There is a bar and restaurant on site so even though it is remote you can eat a nice dinner here (during the season). A few tables situated outside let guests take in the views over the water. Full Irish breakfast cooked to order in the morning.

Doubles from 70€.

http://www.bunbeghouse.com/

Rossnowlagh

The Smugglers Creek Inn

Perched on a cliff high above the beach, this is a unique and special place to stay. Be sure to ask for Room 4, which is tiny, but has a large patio overlooking the beach. You can plant yourself here for hours with a drink and enjoy the sunset, or sunrise, or any time of day. There is a nice restaurant and bar on the ground floor, you will want to make a reservation in high season as this place is wildly popular.

Room 4 from 46€/per person, other rooms from 37€/per person.

http://smugglerscreekinn.com

Buncrana

St Bridget's B&B

Homey, cozy little B&B within walking distance of the pubs and shops in Buncrana town.

Full Irish breakfasts cooked to order in the beautiful little breakfast room.

Double rooms from 80€.

https://www.facebook.com/st.bridgetsguesthouse/

Malin More

Glencolmcille Woollen Mill Shop

A lovely little family-run shop, carrying locally sourced, hand loomed Donegal wool. This is the home of Rosslan Knitwear, whose goods are knit in the workshop on site.

Hours: Open every day 9:30 - 6, open till 7 in the summer. There is a cafe on site where you can get a coffee, tea, and a snack.

http://www.rossanknitwear.ie/

Bridgend

Harry's Bar Farmer's Market

Every Saturday morning, Harry's Bar uses their parking lot to create space for local food producers to share their products. There is a bread baker, a pastry baker, a butcher, a fishmonger, fruit and vegetable stalls. All local, all top quality. This is an excellent place to pick up some amazing food, and have a chance to meet the people who make it.

https://www.facebook.com/Harrys-Restaurant-287755862602/

Sights are free to enter unless otherwise noted.

Creevykeel Tomb, Rossnowlagh beach, Caldragh cemetery, Malin Beg, Glengesh Pass, Cloghanmore, Malin More, Arranmore Island, Beltany stone circle, Fahan Mura cross slab, Mamore Gap, Malin Head, Clonca church and high cross, Norrhburg Castle,

Donegal

Donegal Castle

The castle has several floors you can explore, with lots of signs and displays throughout detailing important history of the region.

Open every day 10-6. Admission 4€. Reduced prices for seniors and students.

http://www.heritageireland.ie/en/northwest/donegalcastle/

Blaney

Tully Castle

The castle is only open Sundays from 12 - 6 (admission is free), but it's worth a visit even if you can't go inside. You can still walk the beautiful grounds, and there are picnic benches nearby.

Glencolmcille

Glencolmcille Folk Village

A collection of replicas of thatched-roof homes that are re-created to show exactly how people from the area lived over the centuries.

Oen Easter Saturday - September 30. Monday - Saturday 10 -6, Sunday 11 - 6.

Admission: Adults 5€, reduced prices for seniors, children, and groups .

http://www.glenfolkvillage.com/

Grainan of Aileach

The site itself (which is incredible, absolutely a must-see destination), is free to enter. Nearby there is a visitor center, which is open Monday - Friday 10:30 - 5:30, and Saturday and Sunday 11 - 5:30. Admission 3€ per person.

ROUTE #5

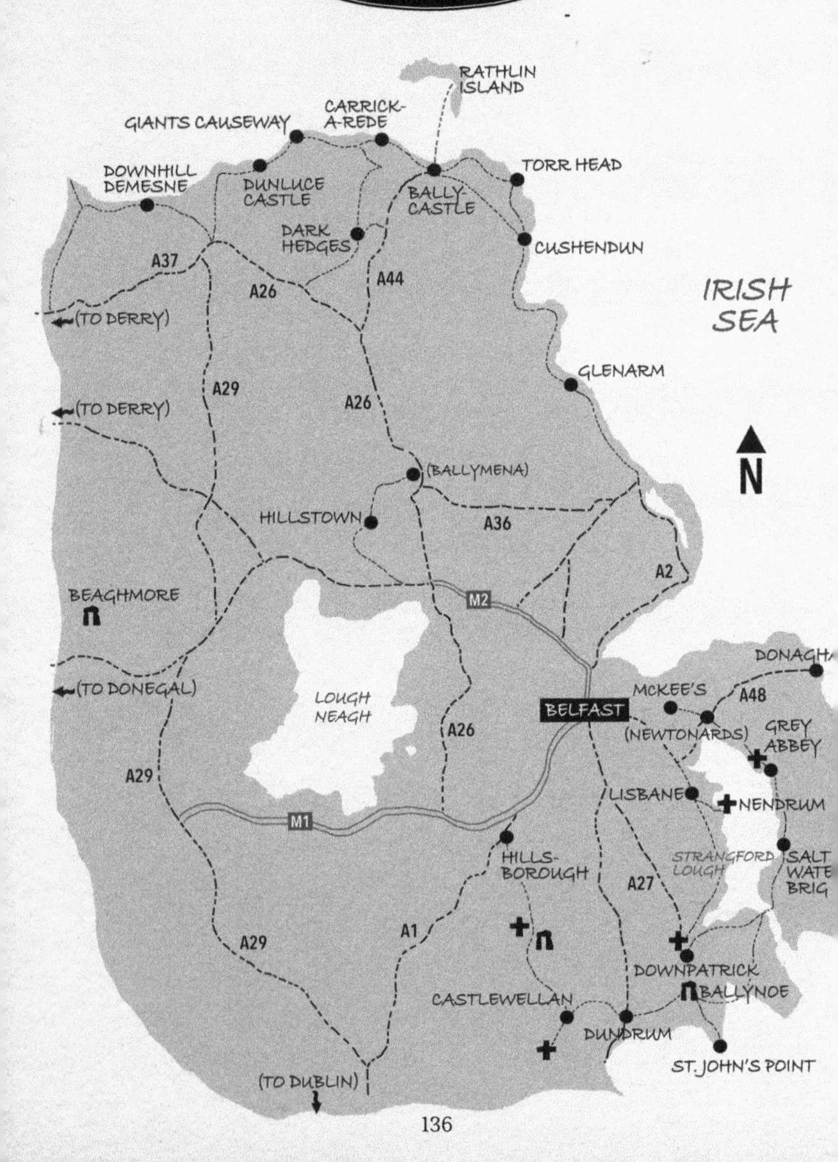
RATHLIN ISLAND
GIANTS CAUSEWAY
CARRICK-A-REDE
DOWNHILL DEMESNE
DUNLUCE CASTLE
BALLY-CASTLE
TORR HEAD
DARK HEDGES
CUSHENDUN
A37
A26
A44
IRISH SEA
(TO DERRY)
(TO DERRY)
A29
A26
GLENARM
(BALLYMENA)
N
HILLSTOWN
A36
A2
BEAGHMORE
M2
(TO DONEGAL)
LOUGH NEAGH
BELFAST
MCKEE'S
A48
(NEWTONARDS)
GREY ABBEY
A26
A29
LISBANE
NENDRUM
M1
HILLS-BOROUGH
STRANGFORD LOUGH
A27
A1
A29
DOWNPATRICK
BALLYNOE
CASTLEWELLAN
DUNDRUM
ST. JOHN'S POINT
(TO DUBLIN)

Northern Ireland

Though Northern Ireland is politically a distinct country and part of the United Kingdom (as opposed to the Republic of Ireland, which the rest of the island comprises), we include it in this book as part of Ireland's geography rather than its politics. Northern Ireland uses British pounds (£) rather than euros (€), and measures distances in miles rather than kilometers. Visitors will be glad to know, however, that here a pint is still a pint, and a Guinness is still a Guinness.

This is a charming part of Ireland, with green hills covered with prized sheep and cows, majestic castles on rocky cliffs, ruins of medieval monasteries and even more ancient stone circles, all of which can make visitors feel like you're on the set of *Game of Thrones*—and not without reason.

Crossing the River Foyle, which to the north becomes the large Lough Foyle (though again, it's a large sea harbor, not a lake), you'll enter the large town of Derry or Londonderry (depending on who you ask). The city is full of history, lovely in places... and a bit large for a Little Roads experience. Follow the A2 highway east. Just before Limavady, turn north on the road marked as the "Causeway Coastal Route" (so-called for reasons that will become obvious later), which winds from Derry all the way to Belfast. On the way you might take a quick detour out to Magilligan Point, which reaches back northwest across Lough Foyle to almost touch the Inishowen peninsula at Greencastle (see previous itinerary).

At this point begins a long stretch of beach reaching east to **Downhill Demesne**. "Demesne" is an old, fancy word for "estate of some rich guy". The rich guy in this case was the eccentric Frederick Hervey, the Fourth Earl of Bristol and Bishop of Derry, better known as simply the "Earl Bishop", a *bon vivant*, art collector, scholar, philanderer, deist (despite being a bishop), and amateur architect. He designed several buildings on this coastal highland property to create the estate, including his mansion (now just a shell, but still fascinating), a mausoleum, a series of carefully planned gardens, and the stunning **Mussenden Temple**.

In recent years Northern Ireland has gained a new degree of notoriety (and therefore an increase in visitors), as it is the filming location for many scenes from the HBO series *Game of Thrones*. This "temple" appears in one such scene, viewed from the beach below. Actually built as a summer library, it is perched literally on the edge of the cliff, so close that the windows on one side look straight down a sheer cliff face to the rocky surf 120 feet below.

The Downhill grounds cover 147 acres, and every step of the many walking paths throughout is worthwhile. Allow yourself a good couple of hours to explore everything this site has to offer. Tickets to this site also grant admission to the nearby historic **Hezlett House**, a surviving 17th-century thatched cottage. Here visitors can learn about what life was like for the people of the time who didn't happen to have the good fortune (as did Hervey) to be born into aristocratic privilege.

To continue east, you have to cross the River Bann in Coleraine. From there, return to the coastal drive by following signs to Portrush, and proceed to the evocative **Dunluce Castle**, perched like a fantasy movie set on a rocky cliff outcropping. Parts of the castle were built as early as the 13th century, on the remains of an early Irish fort. The MacQuillan clan improved it in the 15th century, but the more powerful MacDonnell family soon took it over and established a family supremacy that persists to this day – the current Lord and Lady Dunluce are MacDonnells, residents of another castle we'll come to a bit further down the road. This is a ticketed museum site. Inside, visitors can learn about the history and the legends attached to the castle, as well as explore the ruins.

Another river, the Bush, blocks the coastal path east, so head to the crossing in Bushmills.

This is the home of the famous Bushmills distillery. If you like whiskey and want to enjoy it in the company of busloads of strangers taking pictures, stop here for a tour. Otherwise, continue back to the coast along the Causeway route. This leads to the **Giant's Causeway**, a UNESCO World Heritage Site and one of Ireland's most famous and most visited destinations.

The identity of the "builders" of this strange array of some 40,000 hexagonal pillars interlocked in the surf eluded mankind for eons. A popular legend held that a giant named Finn McCool built it in a competition with a Scottish rival across the water. The more plausible origin story, sorted out in the 18th century and refined since then, is that these geometrical stepstones were freakishly formed as a result of volcanic activity around 50-60 million years ago. The entire site encompasses a mile-long stretch of rocky beach and ocean cliffs, a portion of which is dominated by these unique formations. It is easy to see why ancient (and even Renaissance) people looked to the supernatural realm to explain how such a thing came into being.

This site has an extensive visitor center, which outlines in great detail the geological, legendary,

Finn McCool

Many colorful characters occupy the annals of Irish mythology–knights, witches, pirates, kings, and queens. Finn McCool (ar Anglicization of *Fionn mac Cumhaill*) was a legendary warrior, sometimes portrayed as a giant. Popular legend has it that he built a path o stepping stones to cross the water to Scotland to fight a rival gian there. When Finn saw that the other guy was a lot bigger, he ran bac and begged his wife to help him hide. She obliged, disguising Finn as a baby; when the Scottish giant saw him, he in turn fled back across th stones, fearing that if the baby was that big, the father must be huge and historical features of the place; it also has a huge parking lot suitable for tour buses, and they'll be here in force, especially in high season. Be mindful of the time of day and the time of year when visiting. This is a good place to approach at dawn (the same way we visit the Cliffs of Moher in Itinerary 2).

A bit farther east along the coast are the ancient ruins at **Dunseverick Castle**. Here the remains of an Iron Age fort (around 500 BC) sit on the edge of the cliffs, alongside ruins of various structures from the 8th to the 17th centuries. Intrepid hikers can enjoy a beautiful five-mile coastal path walk from here west to the Giant's Causeway.

Leaving the A2 highway, take the B15 to stay close to the coast. You'll soon come to the entrance of **Carrick-a-Rede** rope bridge park. Salmon fishermen built the original rope bridge here some 350 years ago to take advantage of the spawning route that flowed right by the tiny Carrickarede Island just offshore. Today, visitors without acrophobia can cross over the rushing waters and look down at the surf pounding the ancient caves and cliff edges nearly 100 feet below. Even without the crossing, the short walk out to the bridge leads along a beautiful and scenic stretch of coastal cliffs.

Departing the coastal route for a diversion to the south leads to another *Game of Thrones* location, the **Dark Hedges**. This road has a fairytale quality, lined with overarching beech trees with twisted silvery branches. The trees were planted in the 18th century to create an impressive approach to the Georgian mansion of Gracehill. The manor is now a golf course, but the avenue lead-

ing up to it still maintains its magic atmosphere, especially at dusk or when it is foggy.

From here, make your way southeast across the countryside to the sleepy little harbor town of **Glenarm**, where the aforementioned Lord and Lady Dunluce reside at Glenarm Castle. The castle grounds are occasionally open for tours, as is its beautiful walled garden. The most striking element of the castle is its guard tower, called the Barbican. This imposing gatehouse guards the original entrance to the estate, at the end of a small bridge spanning the Glenarm River. The Glenarm estate includes a farm that produces award-winning organic beef and lamb, and it is also the home to an organic salmon hatchery, whose premium product is sold worldwide. It's also available on a plate at the **Glenarm Castle Garden and Tearoom**. You can spend a lovely hour or two with a snack here and then a stroll through the beautiful gardens.

In town, check out the gallery of **Steenson's Jewellers**. This family-run goldsmith's shop has been in business for 40 years; they pride themselves on producing innovative jewelry with the highest levels of craftsmanship. Their signature pieces include "landscape" jewelry, particularly depicting the Giant's Causeway. They have recently gained international fame as the makers of much of the jewelry seen on *Game of Thrones*.

The aforementioned **Barbican tower**, another Irish Landmark Trust property, is more than a perfect postcard backdrop; it also serves as a lodging for visitors. Booking this place lets you drive across the river bridge through its imposing double doors into the castle grounds. The tower is a fully furnished apartment. Its best feature being a rooftop patio from which guests can enjoy views of the castle, the town, the harbor and the sea beyond.

Glenarm is also a good point to explore this northeast corner of the coast. Take the A2 coast route north. This road runs along the water's

edge, hugging the cliffside for miles. On the way, you'll pass the old church ruin at **Ardclinis**, a 14th-century monastic settlement, surrounded by a graveyard with family burial stones dating from three centuries ago. In the middle of the churchyard stands a hawthorn tree. These were commonly grown at sacred sites like this, another tradition left over from the pagan religions. Today they're considered "wishing trees", where travelers hang ribbons or other talismans in the hope of picking up some good vibes.

Farther north, off the highway, is the cliffside town of **Cushendun** and its nearby coastal caves, yet another *Game of Thrones* location. From Cushendun, take the little route marked as the **Torr Head** scenic route. This is one of our favorite stretches of road anywhere. Narrow and winding, and sometimes blocked by sheep, it climbs the remote cliffs for views of sweeping pastures hosting different breeds of sheep and cows (as well as foxes and Irish hares) and wide expanses of ocean meeting the sky. The Torr Head point itself is the apex of the drive before the descent back to the A2 highway, whose full two lanes will now seem like a U.S. interstate compared to what you've just been driving.

Proceed north on to Ballycastle. Just before the town stands the remains of the 15th-century **Bonamargy Friary**, around which hovers a leg-

endary tale. Another choice piece of real estate built by the MacQuillan family and later seized by the powerful ruling MacDonnell family, this friary somehow withstood the "Dissolution" (i.e., pillaging and destruction) wrought by King Henry VIII in the mid-1500s. Though it was in the hands of the MacDonnells since the 1550s, it was still the home of the famous "Dark Julia" MacQuillan. Known also as the "Black Nun", she was regarded as a mystic and prophetess whose predictions were always dire. Legend has it that she died on the stairs inside the friary, and she still haunts them to this day. At one end of the nave, a gravestone topped with a distinctive holed disc marks her final resting place.

In **Ballycastle**, bikers and foot passengers can take a ferry to **Rathlin Island**, the northernmost point of Northern Ireland. Plan on a whole day to explore this beautiful and solitary place, and appreciate the dedication and the love of the land that was and is required to live in such a remote

location. Bikers will love traversing the mostly empty roads here (foot passengers can hire rental bikes), and hikers will enjoy the many signposted walking trails. The island is steeped in history: The first Viking raid on Ireland landed here in the 8th century, and in 1306 the Scots king Robert the Bruce escaped the clutches of the English army by fleeing across the Scottish Sea to hide out in a cave on the northern sea cliffs. (Scotland is a close 13 miles from here. The MacQuillan and MacDonnell families were both closely tied to Scotland and assisted Robert in his struggles.) About seven miles long end-to-end, little Rathlin is home to some 150 people, a few of whom are scientists at the **Rathlin West Light Seabird Centre**. Birders on foot, bike, or bus will want to visit here, at the site of the old lighthouse on the western end of the island. The cliffs are nesting and breeding grounds aswarm with thousands of seabirds, including the rare Atlantic puffin.

To the south of Glenarm is the city of Belfast. To steer clear of its traffic and crowds, we turn inland toward the large Lough Neagh. Look for **Hillstown Farm Shop** southwest of Ballymena, a beautiful shop selling their own products (they raise chickens and llamas, among other animals) and many locally produced goods – from meat, eggs, and produce to baked goods, jams, and even local beer. A small coffee shop next door makes lovely lunch plates with those same farm goods. Stock up on groceries on the way to a self-catering lodging (like the Barbican). A huge box of food for several days' worth of meals (including beer, apple juice, sausages, cheese, eggs, and snacks of all kinds) will cost maybe 50 bucks, and it's a bonus to know that the food is all local and of such high quality and freshness. This is a great way to eat in Ireland, supporting local farmers and getting the best that this agrarian land has to offer. (Another bonus: You get to watch the action in the corral out in front of the shop, where a couple of llamas vie for space with a handful of chickens.)

If you've come this far inland and have another hour to spare, head a bit farther west to find the extensive **Beaghmore Stone Circles** Neolithic site. These cover an acre or so on a hill surrounded by peat bogs. Indeed, it was workers cutting peat moss for fuel who uncovered the stone formations in the 1930s. The site consists of seven stone circles and 12 stone burial cairns, all with rows of stones in the same alignment. The circles and cairns date from around 1600 B.C., but the site was in use by even earlier people, more than 1000 years previously, who probably cleared and farmed the hillside. ("Beaghmore" probably means "birch forest", suggesting that the place was wooded at one time.) Today the area is desolate, remote, and chilly even on a summer day.

Looping around the south part of Lough Neagh, head back east to the town of **Hillsborough**. In this colorful, quaint, and bustling town you'll find many locally owned shops and a teeming nightlife at its several excellent pubs. Its Forest Park, highlighted by the fort, the lake, and the imposing St. Malachy's Church, makes for a beautiful stroll or an afternoon of people-watching. The town is also an important center for the U.K. government. The castle at the top of the town houses Northern Ireland's Secretary of State and occasionally also the royal family. The castle grounds are open to visitors. Paths traverse vast acres of beautifully maintained gardens, a lake, and woods, including what residents claim is Europe's largest rhododendron.

Hillsborough has two excellent eateries. The local favorite and the oldest one in town dating to 1752 is **The Hillside**, located on Hillsborough's main street, on, of course, the hillside. In summer, a flower-filled beer garden invites drinkers to while away the hours. In winter, open log fires in the pub warm the feet as the whiskey warms the insides. Down the road a bit is the elegant **Parson's Nose**, well known in Hillsborough and all over Northern Ireland as an excellent gastro-pub. The menu changes daily and employs locally sourced, seasonal ingredients. Located in an 18th-century

Georgian townhouse, the pub is cozy and charming, with open fires in one dining room and views over Hillsborough Castle's lake in another. The most interesting place to stay in town is a little holiday rental, the **No. 33 Coach House**, so named because it used to be the coach house of the castle. The property is on the main street, abutting the castle grounds. Local florist Lorna Brownlee is the caretaker for the place, and her green thumb and knack for interior design make it adorable and welcoming. The rooms and patio are bursting with flowers, and the kitchen is stocked with juice, heese, eggs, butter, milk, biscuits, bread, cereal, tea and coffee. Staying here, you'll feel like one of the locals from 100 years ago. Better still, unlike the original residents, you don't have to drive the royals around.

South of Hillsborough are two expansive park attractions, the woodland acres of Tullymore Park, and Castlewellan Forest Park. These offer a plethora of activities for the price of a parking fee (£5 per car), including a hedge maze, miles of hiking/biking trails, a Victorian castle, and a 250-year-old arboretum. For a quieter, less touristy experience, there are several old sites in the area. On the way from Hillsborough, look for **Legananny Dolmen**, a megalith dating from around 2000-2500 BC. Named for Áine (or Anya), a mother-goddess figure, Legananny is capped with an improbably large rock slab supported by three unusually slender stones. Not far from here is the **Finnis Souterrain**, one of many such Iron Age structures in Northern Ireland. Unlike the mystical/astronomical stone circles and other ancient megaliths, these souterrains (literally

meaning "underground") were built to protect residents and their goods from inclement weather and invaders. They consist of an underground network of tunnels and chambers, built with an amazing degree of know-how. This one probably dates from the early (5th century) Christian period. The site is gated to deter the many local sheep, but it's unlocked and open to visitors. A series of solar-powered lights illuminate the depths of the tunnel and chamber, for hardy souls who fear neither spirits nor close spaces.

Another souterrain is southwest of Castlewellan on the narrow but memorably-named Moneyscalp Road, underneath the stone fort of

Drumena Cashel. It's hard to spot. From the road, its stone fortifications blend perfectly with the miles of pasture walls, but a quick walk up the little path to this early-Christian-era site is well worth the trouble. The enclosure is well more than 100 feet in diameter, with walls more than 10 feet thick. Better yet, there is a large underground shelter, the souterrain, which provided protection for the settlement's residents. It is extensive, with several chambers in which the average person of that time period could easily stand upright.

On the way back east, off the B180 road is **Maghera Church and Round Tower**, on the site of an early Christian monastic settlement from the 6th century. The "new" church here is almost 200 years old, situated on a plot where the ruins of a 13th-century church lurk in the background, surrounded by gravestones enclosed by a circular stone wall. Even older still is the ghostly shell of a round tower, dating from at least as far back as the 10th century.

To the east along the coast, seek out the ruins of **Dundrum Castle**, on a hillside overlooking Dundrum Bay on the Irish Sea. Built by the famous and powerful John de Courcy, it is one of a series of coastal fortifications that solidified Anglo-Norman control of this part of Ireland in the 12th century. Hugh de Lacy, another of the Norman heroes (or villains, depending on whose side you were on) who conquered Ireland, later added a tall, circular keep within the walls. The idea of a round keep was relatively new in the 13th century. It was a defensive improvement borrowed from Welsh builders. Today, visitors can climb the spiral stairwell to the top of this tower to enjoy sweeping 360-degree views, making the castle's strategic significance most apparent. It offers a superior vantage point for the Dundrum Bay and the surrounding hillsides and roadways.

The castle is at the heart of the **Dundrum Castle Woods**, a 7.5-acre natural preserve that was planted some 200 years ago by the Marquis of Downshire. A series of footpaths and bike trails weaves through the countryside and to the nearby town, enabling more active visitors to delve into the natural habitat of the local flora and fauna.

Not far from Dundrum is the large megalithic site of **Ballynoe Stone Circle**. It's hard to find, but worth it. A walk through a tree-covered tunnel path brings you to a 5000-year-old circle formation comprising more than 50 stones.

A diversion to the southeast leads to **St John's Point**, where stands a distinctive black-and-yellow lighthouse built in 1844. (The keepers' cottages here are available as holiday rentals from Irish Landmark National Trust.) On the way you'll pass the remains of a tiny church, built a thousand years ago, give or take a century. Like many such religious places, this one was built on the grounds of an earlier religious site, possibly a small monastic settlement. It includes a holy well that has not, perhaps due to the remoteness of the location, become adorned with ribbons and other talismans by pilgrims. Next to the well is a "bullaun", a common element at these ancient religious sites. This is a hollowed-out rock of indeterminate purpose. It may have been placed to collect rainwater for drinking or for use as holy water, or the clergy may have used it as a mortar stone for grinding curative (or recreational?) herbs.

Proceeding north on the A2, you'll come to the town of Strangford and the entrance to the large Strangford Lough, another "lake" that is really a harbor. A 10-minute ferry ride takes you across the strait to Portaferry at the tip of **Ards Peninsula**. Drive up the peninsula on the A20 and grab a pint or a meal at the **Saltwater Brig**, where the menu is handwritten every day on a chalkboard, and the plates are based in tradition and prepared from scratch. The pub's name refers to the nearby bridge over the Blackstaff River. At high tides, the

salty seawater flows upstream. Be sure to ask what's fresh that day. This close to the sea and the lough, the seafood will be as fresh as it gets. The building dates from the late 1700s, when it was a coaching house for travelers going from Portaferry to Belfast.

Further up the Ards peninsula, you'll come to the little village of **Greyabbey**, imaginatively named for the now-ruined 12th-century **Grey Abbey** on the edge of town. The abbey is a large site, and many of its features remain intact. It is thought to be the first Gothic architecture in Ireland, as evidenced by its pointed window arches and other structural details. The site is extensively signposted with a lot of information about the medieval monastic culture therein, bringing the ancient stone ruins to life. The entry passes through a carefully maintained monks' garden, aromatic with countless flowers and herbs. In the town of Greyabbey, look for the charming little alcove of the **Hoops Courtyard**, home to a few local shops, artists' studios, and a café.

All along the drive up Ards, you'll see the silhouette of a tower to the north, looming over the lough. This is Scrabo Tower, built in the 19th century at the edge of the town of Newtownards to look out over all of County Down. Its surrounding park acreage is open to the public, though the tower itself is often closed.

A bit farther north is one of the region's favorite food-lovers' destinations: **McKee's Farm Shop**, an extensive and bustling place with a large grocery section featuring all manner of foodstuffs from local producers, including prepared foods and a butcher's counter. The McKee family l ovingly farms cattle, chickens and eggs, and a variety of produce, all healthily and sustainably grown. The shop has an attached cafe, which is always busy, with made-from-scratch food that's excellent, and sourced locally, of course! Don't miss their cinnamon scones, which are legendary in these parts.

To the east at the coast is the busy little harbor town of **Donaghadee** and its lighthouse and huge stone quay, both from the 19th century. Among the colorful buildings along the harbor's edge is the **Pier 36 Restaurant and Guest House**. The restaurant downstairs is a popular spot for the locals as well as visitors. The rooms upstairs enjoy views out over the harbor; ask for #1, the "Smith Room". It's dedicated to Edward Smith, captain of the RMS Titanic, which was built nearby in the shipyards of Belfast. Down the street is an excellent eatery, **Grace Neills**, where a modern restaurant lies behind what claims to be the oldest pub in Ireland, dating from 1611. Hint: For a more colorful experience, ask to sit for your meal in the historic pub area. Same great food, but in a centuries-old setting.

Before getting any closer to the traffic of Belfast, circle back south on the west side of Strangford Lough on the A22. Along the way is the **Poachers Pocket**, an upscale but casual gastropub in the village of Lisbane. This restaurant has a tiny shop in the front, selling local food products and produce. It's worth noting that the same culinary entrepreneurs at the Parson's Nose in Hillsborough run this place as well, a testament to Northern Ireland's food culture.

A 15-minute-long meander to the east leads along a series of tiny islands connected by a small causeway road. The last is Mahee Island, on which

sits the remains of the monastic settlement of **Nendrum**. This was a hilltop monastery with a large walled enclosure; much of the wall outline is still intact. The bottom of a round tower hints at what once would have been a fantastic view of the Strangford Lough. The remains here include a church, several domestic buildings, and a reconstructed sundial from the 9th century. The monks here were savvy engineers, even in the seventh century. Archaeologists have discovered remnants of an ingenious dam system by which incoming tidal water was captured and then released to turn turbines, providing power to the monastery for its mills. This tidal mill was the earliest such system in the world, built at the time of the settlement in the 7th century. Even then, Ireland was at the forefront of developing renewable energy sources.

Returning back to the mainland, proceed south to the town of **Downpatrick** and the 15th-century **Down Cathedral** that sits atop the hill above the town. As this is purportedly the burial place of not just Saint Patrick—a stone marker denotes "the spot"—but also that of Columba and Brigid (or Brigit), countless throngs of religious pilgrims flock to this location to venerate Ireland's "big three" saints. The cathedral is surrounded by a lush grove that was planted in the 18th century.

Take a drive down the hill out of Downpatrick, and across the Quoile River to the remains of **Inch Abbey**, a 12th-century Cistercian monastic settlement. It was built with the support of the aforementioned John de Courcy, possibly to ease his

Saint Patrick

The elevation of Patrick to his venerated status in Ireland is tinged with irony, since he was in fact a north Britishman, captured by an Irish raiding party in the 5th century and forced to work in the north of Ireland as a shepherd. He wholeheartedly embraced Christianity in response to the paganism of his captors. After he escaped to Europe, he felt a calling to return to Ireland and establish churches there. He became so popular that his subsequent followers must have found it easy to give him credit for driving the snakes out of Ireland. (They were conveniently unaware that glacial movement over the previous 10,000 years saw to it that no snakes at all were in Ireland to begin with.)

guilt over the destruction of another monastery in his invasion of Ireland. (De Courcy supposedly also interred the remains of Brigid and Columba at the Downpatrick site, possibly part of the same contrition.) Inch Abbey was built on an island in the river, which suited the Cistercian preference for solitude. While the river's course has changed over centuries and the site is no longer an island, the sense of seclusion and quiet remains. Sit at this site and look across the marshes—from here you can take in a postcard-perfect view of Down Cathedral—and enjoy the distance you've put between yourself and the crowds of tourists and pilgrims. This sight makes a perfect Little Roads experience.

Note: As of this writing, the border between Northern Ireland and the Republic of Ireland is open and free on all roads, large and small. However, it remains to be seen how travel here will be affected by the "Brexit" vote of

2016, in which the U.K. declared its wish to split from the European Union (of which Ireland is a member). It's also worth noting that Northern Ireland voted narrowly (about 55%-45%) to remain in the E.U.

WHERE TO EAT

Restaurants are open every day for lunch and dinner unless otherwise noted.

Hillsborough

The Hillside

Established in 1752, this is Hillborough's oldest pub. Today it's a restaurant and pub with seasonal menus serving excellent food, much of it locally sourced.

http://www.hillsidehillsborough.co.uk/

The Parson's Nose

Upscale gastropub serving absolutely incredible food, this is a place not to miss. Menu changes often; ask the staff for recommendations, as they are intimately familiar with the menu.

http://www.ballooinns.com/the-parsons-nose

Kircubbin

Saltwater Brig

Good pub food and excellent homemade chowder. If the weather is nice there is an expansive patio where you can enjoy views of Strangford Lough. This is a family-run place and they take great pride in the pub, and are extremely friendly as well.

http://www.saltwaterbrig.com/

Donaghadee

Grace Neill's Pub

Grace Neill's has been open since 1611. Today it's a well-known gastro pub serving excellent traditional Irish fare. The front two rooms are the original 1611 structure; the back is a larger, more modern addition.

http://www.graceneills.com/

Balloo

The Poacher's Pocket

Upscale, award-winning gastropub in the tiny village of Lisbane. Excellent craft beer and cider list, menu using many locally sourced ingredients. If you like something from the menu you might be able to find it in their attached little shop, which has many artisanal items for sale. Reservations recommended, especially for Sunday lunch.

http://www.ballooinns.com/the-poachers-pocket

Glenarm

Glenarm Castle Walled Garden and Tea Room

A cute, charming little tea room where you can have a coffee and cake or lunch before touring the Castle gardens. A little foyer shop is filled with crafts by local artists. Open Easter - mid October, Monday - Saturday 10 - 5, Sundays 11 - 5.

http://www.glenarmcastle.com/tea-room-gift-shop

Glenarm

The Barbican

Renovated gate tower of Glenarm Castle, now open for guests. Wood burning stove here, and plenty of books, so you can curl up by the fire and read. Full kitchen on the top floor, and best of all, above that, an outdoor patio with gorgeous views of the town and valley.

From 255£ for 2 nights.

http://www.irishlandmark.com

Hillsborough

No. 33 Coach House

Absolutely charming house right on Hillsborough's Main Street, the former coach house of Hillsborough Castle. Working fireplace in the sitting room, and a gorgeous little flowery patio. Caretaker Lorna Brownlee is a florist; she leaves fresh flowers there to greet you, and a fridge stocked with the basics.

From 95£/night with a 2-night minimum stay.

http://www.coachhouse-hillsborough.co.uk/

Donaghadee

Pier 36 Guesthouse

Primarily a restaurant; upstairs there are a few rooms. We recommend the Smith room, which is named for the Edward Smith, Captain of the Titanic. The room is large and has gorgeous views of the Irish Sea, and is decorated with mementos from the Titanic. Full Irish breakfast cooked to order in the morning.

Smith Room, from 99£/night.

http://www.pier36.co.uk/

Sights are free to enter unless otherwise noted.

Dunserverick Castle, The Dark Hedges, Ardclinis, Torr Head drive, Bonamargy Friary, Rathlin Island (and Seabird Centre), Beaghmore stone circles, Legananny Dolmen, Finnis Souterrain, Drumena Cashel, Dundrum Castle, Ballynoe Stone Circle, St. John's Point church, Ards Peninsula, Grey Abbey, Nendrum monastic site, Down Cathedral, Inch Abbey

Castlerock

Downhill Demesne and Hezlett House

Stunning grounds, including temples, dovecotes, coastal walks, and beautiful gardens. Open dawn to dusk. Hezlett House and Downhill Demesne facilities buildings open seasonally, check website for details.

Admission: 5£, discounts for seniors and children.

https://www.nationaltrust.org.uk/downhill-demesne-and-hezlett-house

Bushmills

Dunluce Castle

Beautiful ruins of a 16thC castle built on coastal cliffs. You can pay to tour the castle grounds, but even seeing it from outside (for free) is well worth a stop.

Admission: 5£, discounts for seniors and children.

https://discovernorthernireland.com/Dunluce-Castle-Medieval-Irish-Castle-on-the-Antrim-Coast-Bushmills-P2819/

Ballycastle

Carrick-a-Rede Rope Bridge and The Giant's Causeway

These are both highly touristed, but absolutely stunning. If you visit, go as early as possible to avoid busload of tourists.

https://www.nationaltrust.org.uk/carrick-a-rede
http://www.giantscausewayofficialguide.com/

Glenarm

Glenarm Castle Gardens

Gorgeous, lush gardens; an herb garden, The Mount (a man made spiral-wound hill), yew hedges, espaliered fruit trees, fountains, and sculptures.

Open from April 1 - October. Admission for adults 5£, reduced prices for children.

http://www.glenarmcastle.com/

Randalstown

Hillstown Farm Shop

Set out in the countryside, primarily a butcher's, but the shop has a nice selection of local produce, juice, hard cider, beer, cheese, crackers, and baked goods as well.

Open 9 - 5:30 Monday - Saturday, closed Sunday.

http://hillstownfarmshop.com/

Newtownards

McKee's Country Store and Restaurant

Large farm shop with a large restaurant attached, wildly popular with the locals. Restaurant serves food from their own farm – meat and produce. The shop is quite large, with a huge cheese section, and a wonderful bakery section too. Don't miss the cinnamon scone – it's like a snickerdoodle-scone combination.

Open 8:30 - 5:30 Monday - Saturday, closed Sunday. Restaurant open 9 - 4:30.

http://www.mckeesproduce.com

ROUTE #6

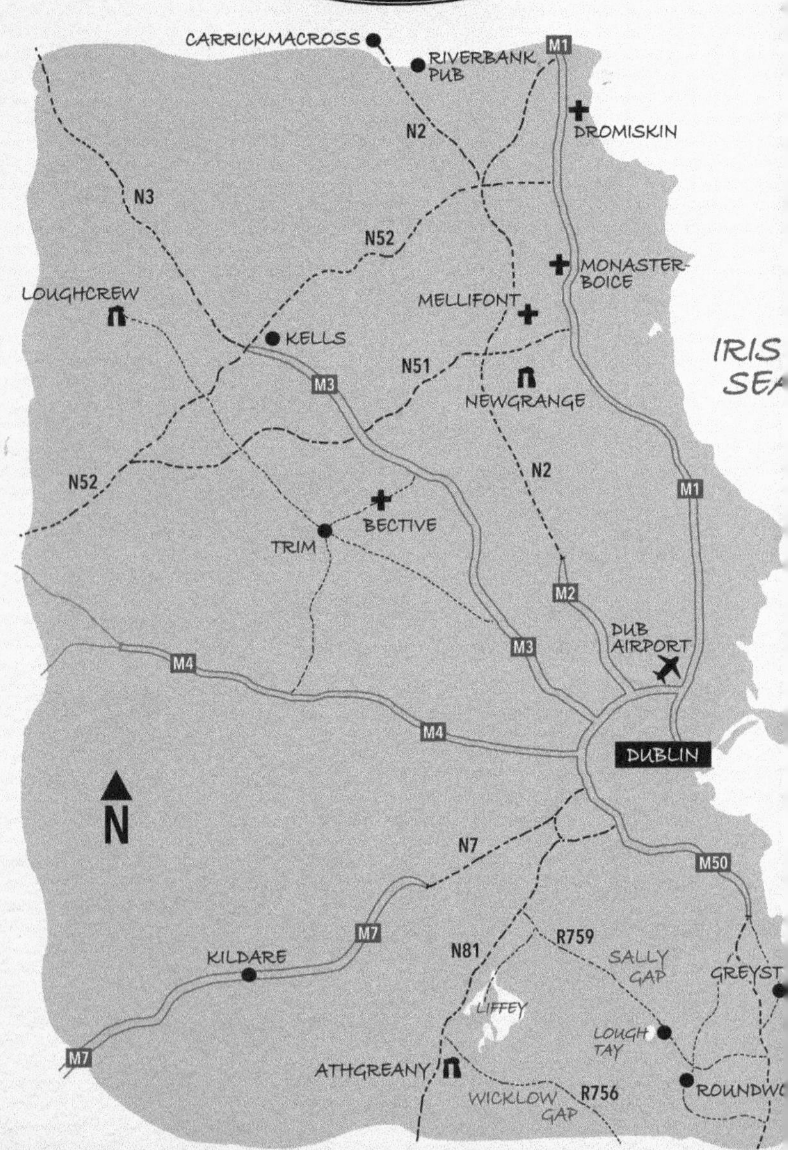
CARRICKMACROSS
M1
RIVERBANK PUB
DROMISKIN
N2
N3
N52
MONASTER-BOICE
LOUGHCREW
MELLIFONT
KELLS
IRIS
SEA
N51
M3
NEWGRANGE
N52
N2
M1
BECTIVE
TRIM
M2
DUB AIRPORT
M3
M4
M4
DUBLIN
N
N7
M50
M7
R759
N81
SALLY GAP
KILDARE
GREYST
LIFFEY
LOUGH TAY
M7
ATHGREANY
ROUNDW
WICKLOW GAP
R756

Eastern Ireland

This itinerary covers a good many of our favorite places of interest within an hour or so of Dublin Airport, making an easy last day before departing or a quick bit of sightseeing when you first arrive. For us, Dublin itself is a "big" city, and despite its famous sights—tourist Meccas such as the Guinness brewery or the Book of Kells at Trinity College—we always opt to head out on the little roads into the countryside.

To the northwest of Dublin is the town of **Trim**, most famous for **Trim Castle**. Fans of *Braveheart* will want to know that this was a filming location for the movie. Built in 1173, this Norman castle is the biggest of its kind in Ireland. Much remains intact or preserved, including the massive keep, a wall, a moat, and several ancillary buildings. The castle was accessible by river from Dublin and therefore the rest of the world. It was on the outskirts of the "Pale", the area of Norman/Anglo control centered in Dublin. Those in the "Pale" stood against the vast power of the Gaelic Irish that lay "beyond the Pale", from whence comes the expression describing something that has just gone too far.

We highly recommend taking the guided tour of Trim Castle (which is, in any case, the only way to see the inside), which details the history and structure of the castle. Within walking distance to the castle is the lodging at **Highfield Guest House**, a former maternity hospital built in 1834. Hostess Geraldine Duignan can offer a variety of suggestions on where to eat in town, what music is on that night, and where to visit nearby.

One of our favorite places near Trim is the eerie ruin of **Bective Abbey**, up the R161 road. Despite it being another *Braveheart* filming location, this 12th-century Cistercian abbey is our favorite kind of site. There's no parking area. From the

road you have to go through a farm gate and across a short stretch of pasture (so watch your step!), and then you must climb over a stile in the wall to get into the abbey grounds. It's not a large site, just the wall and a few buildings, but just try exploring these ancient stones and then say you don't believe in ghosts.

Another monastic settlement lies farther north, directly off the M1: **Monasterboice**, where you'll see one of the best examples of the iconic Irish round towers and Celtic high crosses. Round towers like the one here were probably bell towers, used also for storage and for protection from raiders—at least from those who didn't have ladders. The crosses are highly decorated with carvings depicting scenes from the Old and New Testaments. This was one way that ancient monks reinforced Biblical tales for their illiterate flock. This settlement was founded around 520 AD.

It was raided by Vikings in the 10th century (apparently they had ladders), and gradually fell into decline after the abbey at nearby **Mellifont** opened in the 12th century. Mellifont, also in ruins, was the first Cistercian abbey in Ireland. North of Monasterboice is the town of **Dromiskin** and its historic church site. The grounds include a 13th-century abbey ruin, the shell of a "newer"

church, and a round tower. The tower is distinctive for its door way, about 13 feet from the ground; it has a double set of columns, at the head of which are carved faces.

South of Monasterboice is the amazing **Newgrange** Neolithic site, part of the Brú na Bóinne (Boyne River Valley) area, which also includes other lesser ancient sites. Newgrange is a passage tomb built around 5000 years ago, predating both Stonehenge and the Pyramids. This is a huge, acre-wide stone megalith with an opening that allows entry deep into the tomb area. The passage is about 60 feet long. Geologists have determined that many of the stones that were used in the building—huge

stones, some of them weighing many hundreds of pounds—came from areas of Ireland that were dozens of miles distant, with no good explanation of how they were transported by "primitive" man. Incredibly, the whole thing was built without mortar. Many of the stones have mystical carvings, some apparently referring to astronomical events of obvious importance to the builders. The opening of the tomb, and the passage within, are built in such a way that a strange thing happens once every year for about 17 minutes. On the Winter Solstice, if it's a clear day at dawn, a shaft of sunlight penetrates the usual pitch-darkness of the tomb and illuminates the entire length of the inner passage, shining a ray of light on an inscribed pattern on one of the central interior stones… at which point we're just one face-melting Nazi stooge away from an Indiana Jones movie scene.

This is a heavily visited site, so they've made visiting tricky in order to control crowds. Rather than driving to the actual edifice itself, you must cross the Boyne River to the south to find the "*Brú na Bóinne* Visitor Centre". The center is a museum, and it has a great deal of information about the history of Newgrange and the science behind it. Buy your tickets here for the next tour. A stroll down a footpath and across a little bridge brings you to a bus that will take your group to the site.

Off to the west is the busy market town of **Kells**, the former "home" of the famous illuminated tome the Book of Kells. The abbey here may be where the book was created, in part, and though the book itself is now at Trinity College, the site is still fascinating. On the grounds of Saint Columba's church looms a 10th-century round tower and several carved high crosses.

Still farther afield to the northwest is a truly ancient site, the calendar-based burial chambers of **Loughcrew Cairns**. Constructed around 3500 BC, they pre-date even Newgrange by several centuries. Loughcrew is a series of stone walls, circles, and tunnels built at the crowns of two adjacent hilltops. The tunnels run in a cruciform pattern underground. Some of the stones at the entrances and within are inscribed with pictograms of mysterious meaning, like those at Newgrange. One of these, at the back of one of the tunnels, becomes illuminated at sunrise on the Autumnal and Vernal Equinoxes. As at Newgrange, the precision in alignment and construction of these megaliths speak volumes to the ingenuity, spirituality, and astronomical understanding of the ancient people of this land. Prehistoric, yes, but hardly primitive.

While this is a far less known and less touristy destination, tour guides do lead visits to these cairns, and they're popular among religious pilgrims and wanderers with druidic leanings, so you may run into a crowd or two here. But in off-season or early in the day you'll likely have the place to yourself. A few miles down the road from the site is a coffee shop, where the shopkeepers will let you borrow the key to unlock the gates protecting the tunnels.

To the north-west is Carrickmacross, a busy town with lots of dining and lodging options. For a unique experience, seek out the **Riverbank Country Pub & Guesthouse**, about 10 minutes to the southeast of town. Here in the quiet countryside you'll find cozy, comfortable rooms, hearty and tasty home cooking, and a lively pub scene that's popular with locals as well as visitors. From here it's about an hour to the Dublin airport, making this a Little Roads-style alternative to a generic airport hotel.

Another 10 minutes to the east from the Riverbank Pub is the town of Louth and the ancient **Saint Mary's Priory**. It was built on a monastic site established in the 6th century by Saint Mochta, a disciple of Saint Patrick. A restored 12th-century house sits in the field nearby. Legend has it that it was built in one night to accommodate Mochta. (No, the timeline there doesn't add up; that's why it's legend.) This abbey had been ravaged many times over several centuries even before Henry VIII "dissolved" it in the 1500s. It contains an eerie trove of carved stonework, ancient half-buried

grave markers, a mysterious stairwell leading underground, and two grass-covered crypts. The church itself is the length of half a football field, among the longest such in Ireland. It must have been impressive indeed when it was intact, 800 years ago. Today, it's all just spooky as hell.

Another 10 minutes to the north from Louth, look for the town of **Inniskeen**. The stump of a round tower squats in a churchyard filled with interesting architecture and gravestones dating at least as far back as the 1600s, and those are just the readable ones. This was the site of a monastery founded in the 7th century. The town is also the birthplace and burial place of the poet

and novelist Patrick Kavanagh, one of the most popular literary figures of Ireland.

Southwest of Dublin down the M1 is the bustling town of **Kildare**. This town is now regrettably known as an outlet-mall paradise (or hell, depending on your disposition). But it was famous for its Cathedral of St Brigid, on whose grounds stands a tall round tower. Indeed, only the one at Kilmacduagh Abbey in Galway (see Itinerary 2) is taller in all of Ireland. Saint Brigid is said to have formed an abbey in Kildare in the 5th century, the remains of which are at the south edge of town near the huge shopping complex.

Despite Kildare's historical importance (and several dining and lodging options, like **Hartes Bar and Grill** and the **Lord Edward Hotel**), the shopping crowds can be overwhelming. You may prefer instead to head directly south of Dublin, near the coast, where you'll find the little town of **Greystones**. On the main street are two excellent eateries. **The Three Qs** is a casual bistro run by the trio of Quinn brothers, hence the name. They combine culinary expertise with local produce and meats to make lovely brunch plates and imaginative international dishes. When we had brunch there one morning, we had to move one of our chairs momentarily to make room for the market guy bringing in a load of fresh vegetables from his truck, so you can trust that what you're

eating is fresh and thoughtfully sourced. Up the street is the storefront of **The Happy Pear**, a café and grocery specializing in vegetarian and vegan dishes, again using local suppliers, and again run by brothers—the twins Dave and Steve Flynn. You'll find their fine food products—jams, salsas, hummus, and more—in shops all over Ireland.

For a more standard pub setting, head southwest, away from the sea and up into the foothills. The tiny village of **Roundwood** is an idyllic setting

where **Byrne & Woods Pub & Restaurant** offers stellar food in a casual atmosphere. Standards like fish & chips or rustic lamb stew share a menu with items like salmon with a basil cream sauce, or a slow-roasted pork belly with sage chutney and a cider jus. The menu changes regularly, and daily specials are determined by the chef according to what's fresh.

From Roundwood, head north and then west on R759 into the Wicklow Mountains. The Wicklow range is the largest in Ireland, and this road to **Sally Gap** is the highest. (It may well be closed in winter, as it's impassible if there's snow or ice.) On the climb you'll see, far down a precipitous hillside, the entirety of **Lough Tay**. The estate of the famous Guinness family is at one end of the lake. Indeed, its dark waters and the light sandy beach strand at its north end makes the lake look very much like a glass of stout, earning it the nick-

name “Lake Guinness”.

At Sally Gap there’s a crossroads with the R115, otherwise known as the Old Military Road. This route traverses the spine of the Wicklow range, and it’s as hazardous as it is scenic. We recom-

mend instead continuing on the R759 down the other side of the mountains and head toward Blessington and Hollywood. You'll eventually come to the straight and wide N81, and you can release your vise grip on the steering wheel. Take this highway south (going north leads straight back to Dublin), and look on the east side for the little brown sign for "Pipers Stones" and the megalith icon. This is **Athgreany Stone Circle**. "Athgreany" may have been a translation of "field of the sun", suggesting, as with many such sites, an astronomical purpose of the circle, but they're referred to colloquially as the Piper's Stones. The legend (not unique to this site – there are several other "Piper's Stones" circles in Ireland and Eng-

land) says that pagan dancers on the site were punished for their revelry by being turned to stone by some killjoy deity. The single large stone outside the circle was their piper. There's an old, twisted hawthorn tree in the circle, suggesting that the site might have been of importance to the (non-petrified) pagan dwellers of the area. Thorn trees like this are common at ancient megaliths. They were associated with folkloric fairies, and were thought to be sources of great magic. Today it has become a "wishing tree", with ribbons hanging on it left by visitors in an effort to capture a bit of enchantment.

A crossroads lies just to the north, at Hollywood. Turn back east on the R756. This is the only other crossing of the Wicklow Mountains. It's also the route marked Saint Kevin's Way. The 6th-

Saint Kevin of Glendalough

Born in 498, Kevin led a life abounding with legends, as laid out in folklore and poetry for centuries afterwards. Most had to do with animals and plants, hence his designation as the patron saint of nature. The most famous of these is the story of a blackbird that came to rest on his outstretched palm and began to build a nest in Kevin's hand. He accommodated the bird until its eggs were laid and hatched. Another tells of Kevin compelling a willow tree to produce apples. A third suggests that Kevin's prayer for help feeding a child was answered by a doe appearing, whom he milked; the doe was eaten by a wolf, so Kevin then compelled the wolf produce milk. This milking-wolf story doesn't explain why he didn't just milk the cow from one of his many other legends, which produced as much as dozens of ordinary cows.

century patron saint of nature purportedly set out from Hollywood (there is a church there dedicated to him) and crossed the mountains over what is now the Wicklow Gap, second only to the Sally Gap road in height. If you're lucky to have a clear day, Wales is visible from the pass. Saint Kevin is said to have descended the mountains, leading him to... our next itinerary.

Restaurants are open every day for lunch and dinner unless otherwise noted.

Roundwood

Byrne and Woods Bar and Restaurant

Fantastic gastro pub in the tiny crossroads town of Roundwood. Everything handmade and made to order. Reservations recommended. Open every day for lunch and dinner, but opening hours depend on the season, so check in to be sure.

http://www.byrneandwoods.com

Carrickmacross

The Riverbank Guesthouse

This gastropub and guesthouse is set in an idyllic countryside setting, about 45 minutes from Dublin's airport. In the same family for four generations, today the pub is absolutely packed with locals looking for a great meal, so reservations are necessary. A perfect place to stay for your last night before flying out.

Open for dinner Wednesday - Saturday. Sundays open for lunch and dinner.

http://www.theriverbank.ie/

Greystones

The Three Q's

Award-winning restaurant in the heart of the small village of Greystones. Often restaurants that serve breakfast, lunch, and dinner are just churning out food, but The Three Q's is making excellent food from scratch, with a lot of attention to quality and detail. Highly recommended.

Open Tuesday - Friday for breakfast, lunch, and dinner; Saturday and Sunday from 9 - 3.

http://www.thethreeqs.com/

Kildare

Harte's of Kildare

Popular and well-known gastropub in the village of Kildare. There is also a cookery school here. Reservations recommended.

Open Tuesday - Sunday for lunch and dinner.

https://harteskildare.ie/

Trim

Highfield Guesthouse

B&B with comfy beds, 'welcome' scones upon arrival, and full Irish breakfasts in the morning. Trim Castle is just down the street.

Doubles from 90€.

http://highfieldguesthouse.com/

Carrickmacross

The Riverbank Guesthouse

See listing in "Where to Eat". Rooms are comfortable and in a peaceful countryside setting.

Doubles from 90€.

Kildare

The Lord Edward

Hotel with bar and restaurant right on the town square of Kildare, a 45 minute drive to Dublin's airport.

Doubles from 90€.

http://lordedwardkildare.ie/

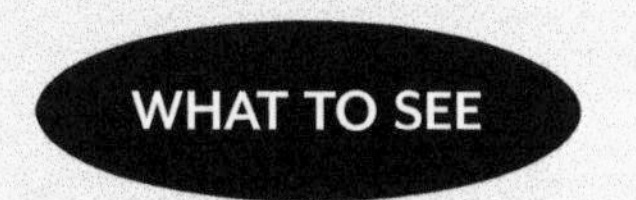

Sights are free to enter unless otherwise noted.

Monasterboice, Bective Abbey, Mellifont Abbey, Dromiskin church and round tower, Loughcrew Cairns, Saint Mary's Priory, Inniskeen round tower, Kildare round tower, Sally Gap, Lough Tay, Athgreany stone circle.

Staleen

Newgrange

Incredible ancient site, open year round. Opening times vary by season, and admission prices vary depending on whether or not you want to see the exhibition center, Newgrange, Knowth, or some combination of all three.

Full information on website: http://www.newgrange.com/

Trim

Trim Castle

Open year round, but hours vary by season so check the website. Admission 5€, discounts for seniors and students.

http://www.heritageireland.ie/en/midlands-east-coast/trimcastle/

Greystones

The Happy Pear

Wonderful little shop specializing in whole food for vegetarians and vegans. When you need a break from steak and Guinness pie, this is the place to go. Their products can be found in many stores across Ireland but their shop is in Greystones. Open Monday - Thursday 8:30 - 6, Friday/Saturday 8:30 - 9, Sunday 10 - 5.

https://thehappypear.ie/

ROUTE #7

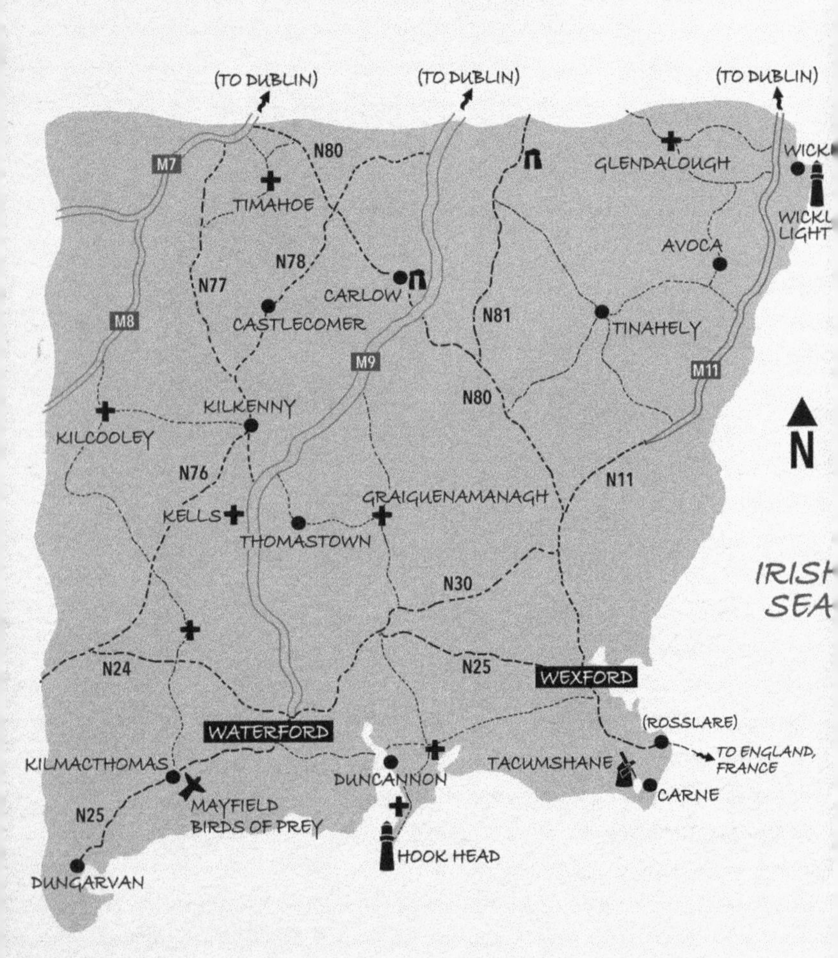

(TO DUBLIN)
(TO DUBLIN)
(TO DUBLIN)
M7
N80
TIMAHOE
GLENDALOUGH
N78
N77
CARLOW
CASTLECOMER
M8
N81
AVOCA
TINAHELY
M9
M11
N80
KILKENNY
KILCOOLEY
N76
N11
N
GRAIGUENAMANAGH
KELLS
THOMASTOWN
N30
N24
N25
WEXFORD
WATERFORD
(ROSSLARE)
TO ENGLAND, FRANCE
KILMACTHOMAS
DUNCANNON
TACUMSHANE
CARNE
MAYFIELD BIRDS OF PREY
N25
HOOK HEAD
DUNGARVAN

Southeastern Ireland

In this area of southeastern Ireland you can stay inside a lighthouse, if you don't mind climbing lots of steps. You can drive on a beach. You can hike to a "secret" seal cove. You can buy beautiful goods at Ireland's oldest working woolen mill. You can explore castles and stone circles, discover ancient round towers and carved high crosses, and wander the empty shells of medieval monasteries. And, of course, you can find farm-grown foodstuffs, eat your fill at fine gastropubs, and try locally made craft brews... or stick with a perfect pint of Smithwicks.

Readers of our previous itinerary who are quivering with anticipation will be glad to learn that the panoramic R756 road that crosses the mountain range at Wicklow Gap leads to the monastic settlement of **Glendalough**. Saint Kevin, it is said, founded the monastery upon his arrival after his trek across the gap in the 6th century. Most of the buildings here are much newer, a mere thousand years old or so. The site is extensive, consisting of a cathedral, several other churches, a 100-foot tall round tower, and cemetery grounds that include several impressive Celtic tall crosses. The nearby lake, aptly named Glendalough, is actually two lakes connected by a stream. The settlement is close to the smaller, lower one, though ancient remains can be found throughout the wood paths. This area is itself part of the Wicklow Mountains National Park area—a fitting setting for the patron saint of nature.

To the east is the lively harbor town of Wicklow, where pubs and shops abound. Stop in for a nice lunch or dinner at the hip **Phil Healy's Pub**, where they offer a lot of local craft brews on tap, good food, and quirky service touches: Your water comes in a carafe, infused with mint. The food is presented artfully, like chips that come in a little metal basket, served with handmade ketchup. Down the street, try a bowl of seafood chowder at the **Bridge Tavern**, a local pub with

lodging rooms and live music every night. Their seafood comes from the fishmonger up the street, the meats come from the local butcher, and their bars (yes, plural) specialize in various Irish whiskeys from around the country.

Saint Kevin of Glendalough, continued

Another legend around the life of 6th-century Saint Kevin tells the story of an old goose who was the beloved companion of a king of the pagans. The king implored Kevin to use his miraculous powers to restore the bird's youth, so he could keep his pet. Kevin agreed, with one condition: That he would be granted whatever lands the goose flew over. The king agreed to this, thinking the goose would never really fly much at all. Kevin exerted his power and restored the goose to its youthful state, and the elated bird took off, soaring over the valley and across two lakes. The king kept to his word and gave Kevin the land, on which he founded the Glendalough monastery.

In the center of town is the **Wicklow Gaol** museum, complete with actors depicting life on the wrong side of the law in past centuries. On the other side of the port, to the south at the edge of town, is a park that's home to the ruins of the 12th-century **Black Castle**. A few cannons are on display in the park, no doubt to highlight the castle's historically strategic position, as it commands a view of the harbor and the coast in both directions.

Following the R750 south out of town soon leads to the most interesting lighthouse we've ever experienced, and it's another Irish Landmark Trust rental property: the **Wicklow Head Lighthouse**, built in 1781. Rather than a set of keepers' cottages, this lighthouse is a single octagonal obelisk standing alone.

The lodging is inside the tower itself. A spiral staircase of 109 steps leads from the ground floor foyer to the kitchen at the top level, which enjoys

360-degree views of, well, everything. Staying here is not for the faint of heart. The winds on these isolated bluffs are constant and strong, whistling or howling all night. But when it comes to unique lodgings, this one is a standout.

A coastal hiking path traverses right by the lighthouse. Following this to the north over the hills and river gullies leads eventually back to

Wicklow town. On the way, look for a little beach cove, where you may see a dozen or more seals basking and, depending on the season, mating. Note: Do NOT approach these animals! They'll act like scared dogs and scatter if they're alarmed. Instead, climb up to the adjacent cliff point, and enjoy a birds-eye view of the herd. They'll see you watching them and warily watch you back, but stay still and quiet and they'll go back to their business of... Well, whatever it is, it's their business, isn't it?

Work your way south on the R754 or R752 roads, which meet at a bridge in the little village of Avoca. The River Avoca here was harnessed centuries ago to create, among other things, the

Avoca handweavers' mill in 1723. The establishment persists today, offering customers the best Irish wool spun into high-quality knit goods. The village was also the set of the popular Irish TV show *Ballykissangel*. You can see the memorabilia (and the oft-used setting of the show) on the walls at **Fitzgerald's Pub**.

From here, pick up the R747 and head west. In these countryside wanderings you'll come upon an assortment of cute towns, including Aughrim, an old granite-industry village. The buildings here all have a distinctive look, as they were built largely from the same granite. Look for the blacksmith's forge, built in 1873, distinguished by its round red door.

Continue west to the town of Tinahely. South of town on the R749, look for **Tinahely Farm**

Shop. Here you will find local cheese, eggs, produce, jams, honeys, meats, and baked goods. There's also a lovely little café and restaurant on site. During the holidays, they have a lot of local Christmas-themed crafts, chocolates, and gifts. A friendly couple own the place, and will happily recommend local sights. For families, the "Activity Barn" offers a lot to do for kids, including "Wicklow's largest indoor beach".

Ireland's sheep, and woolen mills

A few days of driving the back roads of Ireland reveal that sheep are among the most populous residents of the island. Discounting the metropolitan areas of Dublin and Belfast, roughly the same number of sheep and humans live here. Aside from the delicious shepherd's pies on pub menus, these sheep are valuable to the economy for their wool. Many weavers in different parts of the country engage in generations-long traditions of spinning wool to make fine, high-quality knit goods. Look for shops connected to woolen mills, and those near the big wool centres, like the famous Aran Islands on the west coast. But beware of knockoffs—if it seems really cheap, it probably is. You can ask the shopkeepers about who made what and from where.

Follow the R747 farther west to the town of Baltinglass, where there's a 12th-century abbey ruin. Here, take the N81 highway up to the little L4321 road, which leads to **Castleruddery stone circle**. This megalith is a stone circle atop an earthen enclosure, dating from around 2500 BC.

It once had 29 or 30 upright stones in a diameter of about 100 feet, including two huge boulders at one end that probably formed a special entrance portal. Locals refer to this site as the "Druid's Circle". It is aligned geographically and astronomically with other sites in the region, and is believed to emanate healing vibrations. It is therefore a pilgrimage destination, complete with a hawthorn "fairy tree" (typical of these sacred sites) decorated with visitors' ribbons and other talismans.

Another interesting megalith lies to the south, on the R726 just east of the large town of Carlow: the massive and ancient **Brownshill portal tomb**. Probably built earlier than 3000 BC, this tomb has possibly the heaviest capstone (the one balanced

MEMORIAL
LIBRARY

atop the supporting "portal" stones) of any such site in Europe, weighing as much as 150 tons. This would have been the burial site of important Neolithic people, though this particular site has never been excavated.

About a half-hour drive northwest from Carlow will take you to **Timahoe** and its church and round tower. The history of this site goes back to a monastery founded in the 7th century; you'll find artifacts in the churchyard from many periods since then, including ancient church remains. The round tower dates from around 1200 AD and stands nearly 100 feet high. Its high door is carved with a double set of columns. Like the tower door at Dromiskin in the previous chapter, the capitals or "heads" of these columns are elaborately-carved heads.

From here, make your way down to the N77 or N78 highways, and continue on toward Kilkenny. On the N78 you'll pass through Castlecomer, the home of **Susan Boland Ceramics**, one of several artists' studios based in the Castlecomer Discovery Park. The 80-acre activity park arose from an old mining estate; the studios are in the old stables and blacksmith's buildings.

A diversion west into County Tipperary will lead you to one of our favorite medieval sites. Look for Jonestown or Urlingford near the M8 motorway.

Follow R689 south to R690. When approaching the site you'll first pass an 18th-century estate house and a "new" (c. 1870s) parish church. At the edge of the vast property is an old walled family burial plot with an incongruous pyramid structure, apparently a crypt housing the original owners of the estate. Past this is a little lane that leads through a bit of woods to a huge meadow, in the center of which are the extensive ruins of **Kilcooley Abbey**. This Cistercian abbey was founded in 1182 and, like nearly all of its counterparts, it was "suppressed" (that is, raided, looted, and seized by the forces of Henry VIII) in the 1540s. The field outside the abbey has a little round stone building, possibly a dovecote or a guardhouse. The abbey itself is dark and mysterious in places, with a wealth of intricately carved stonework on the walls, doorways, windows, baptismal font, and tombs, in which mythical creatures (including a mermaid) lurk among the more typical Biblical depictions and complex tracery. The lid of one sarcophagous is carved with an effigy of a knight, with a dog at his feet guarding the tomb.

Work your way back to **Kilkenny**, a busy river town, the cultural center of the county, and, perhaps most importantly, the historic home of Smithwicks ale. The town was the family seat of the Butler dynasty, which controlled County Kilkenny from the castle here since the 14th century and is still prominent today. (The knight entombed in Kilcooley was of this line, buried there in 1526.) Today the castle is open for guided tours, though visitors may freely wander the highly kept grounds. Across from the castle is the **Kilkenny Design Centre**. Here, in the castle's old

coach houses and stable buildings, two large shops feature woolen knits, ceramics, paintings, candles, soaps, foodstuffs, jewelry and more from artists all over Ireland. Smaller shops within the courtyard house workshops of artisans, mostly jewelers.

Kilkenny is a large town that has retained much of its historic charm, including the atmospheric pub in the old **Hibernian Hotel**, on the cobbled and charmingly named Pudding Lane. The pub in this upscale hotel (a converted 19th-century bank building) is filled with "old-timey" furniture and decor. The fireplace makes the pub feel like a living room, crackling and toasty on cool days. The food is excellent traditional fare, made in-house. Kick back with a pint and pretend you're an aristocrat in the 1800s. Across the street the **Left Bank Bar** and its upscale restaurant Rive Gauche offer a variety of menus from classic pub fare to fine dining. Up the street a few blocks is the **Marble City Bar**,

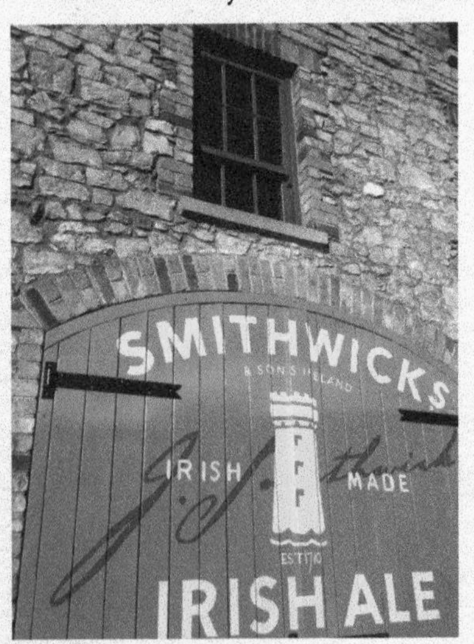

a hip, fun place with great food in the heart of the town's shopping district.

Cross the bridge over the River Nore to find Langton's Hotel, an old family establishment that has grown into an extensive property, including a pub, a café, a restaurant, and the historic and adorable **Bridie's Bar and General Store**. Back in the day, the owner wanted to convert Bridie's from a general store to a pub, but the town council said no, that there were already too many pubs on the street. So the owner kept the front room as a general store, and converted the back room to a bar, as it charmingly remains today.

From Kilkenny, work your way south to the town of Kells. Just to the east of town is the extensive monastic fortification of **Kells Priory**, among

the largest such in Ireland. Covering several acres, the remains of the buildings here represent different eras of development. Augustine friars established the priory near the end of the 12th century on the site of an earlier Norman church. The outlines of the church and cloister walls are still largely intact today, including arched windows and ornately carved stone walls and doorways. Unlike most of these old monasteries, this one was fortified with a 15th-century walled enclosure with guard towers to protect livestock (and other inhabitants) from marauders. Despite these fortifications, the priory failed to resist King Henry's purge in the 1540s.

(This site is not to be confused with the Abbey of Kells, the longtime home of the famous book—see Itinerary 6.)

East of Kells is the little artsy village of **Thomastown**, home to a craft school, a food school, and a wine school. A lot of artists, food professionals, and craftspeople have shops here; grab a cappuccino and a couple of handmade chocolates at the **Truffle Fairy**, where they craft unusual flavors like tequila-lime-salt and orange-cardamom.

A quarter-hour farther east from Thomastown is **Graiguenamanagh**, a town that offers several elements of interesting history: Its ancient Duiske Abbey cemetery holds Celtic high crosses from the 8th and 9th centuries. Just up the street from the Abbey is the small shop of Cushendun Woolen Mills, a 200-year-old family business. Around the corner from the Woolen Mill is a row of old workers' houses, one of which was once home to the O'Leary family, one of whom achieved some notoriety after emigrating to the U.S. and settling in Chicago in the 1800s. (As it turns out, the infamous story of Mrs. O'Leary's cow starting the 1871 Chicago fire was actually a fiction created by a journalist reporting on the conflagration; the idea easily took root in the virulent anti-Irish-immigrant atmosphere in the U.S. at the time.) When you're done exploring the town, pop in for a pint - or maybe buy a new rake - at the old **Mick Doyle's Pub**, which is also a hardware store (or vice-versa).

Almost directly south of Kells on a little unnamed road is the **Kilree monastic site**. This medieval site was built, legend has it, on the remains of a 6th-century monastery founded by Saint Brigid. It's a walled enclosure set in a small grove of trees surrounded on all sides by livestock pasture, and includes a 10th-century church and an 11th-century round tower. In the field just outside the wall, well-guarded by cows, stands a weathered 9th-century High Cross. Its carvings depicting Biblical scenes are typical for that era. These were teaching tools of the clergy to help impart stories to the illiterate populace. The silence of the woods here, the twisty trees, the looming round tower, the ancient burial stones throughout, all conspire to create a spooky atmosphere. When we visited, the cows escorted us out, making us wonder if they were the spirits of ancient monks. While we don't generally believe in such things, that day we did opt for the cheese plate at lunch, rather than the steak and Guinness pie.

Some more intact (and less scary) Celtic crosses overlook the countryside farther south of Kells, off the R697 road at the **Kilkieran Cemetery**. Take the R698 east for a few hundred meters. A walled enclosure surrounds the cemetery on the right. Stone building fragments at this site suggest a church or small monastery. Still prominent are three Celtic High Crosses. Some of their faces are carved with abstract designs and animal figures, like the horsemen that can (barely) be seen on one. In a corner of the cemetery is a poignant marker: the "Stranger's Corner", to honor the unidentified dead. Just down the hill a bit is Saint Kieran's Well, purportedly the source of waters that heal maladies like headaches.

(Note: Little Roads Europe is not responsible for resulting illnesses or hexes from drinking from this.)

All these explorations of dead people may leave travelers wishing for something more... alive. To this end, head south to the town of Kilmacthomas. Here, you can book a session with one of the bird masters at **Mayfield Birds of Prey**, an extraordinary hands-on experience. This takes place in a complex of buildings built during the Famine Years for poor workers; one is a big barn-like room that was originally a church. The facility, long abandoned, has recently been renovated to become the homes for, and displays of, several different owls, falcons, and hawks. Visitors are allowed, with careful supervision, to handle, feed, and even fly some of these beautiful birds. The handler will tell you everything there is to know about these magnificent animals. You can also schedule a "hawk walk", a short hike through the countryside on which the handler lets the birds stretch their wings out over the meadows to show off their flying prowess. Interacting with these gorgeous animals is a singular and memorable experience.

The Mayfield site is directly on the newly-opened Waterford Greenway, a stunning off-road biking/hiking trail and the longest in Ireland. Built on an old railway bed, it stretches 46 kilometers east-west from Dungarvan to Waterford City.

After feeding the birds, you may want to feed yourself—not that previously frozen rodents should whet your appetite. From Kilmacthomas you can pick up the N25 southwest to return to the coast at the harbor town of **Dungarvan**. In the old town center is **Merry's Gastro Pub**. A handwritten chalkboard (always a good sign) displays each day's specials, all freshly made and beautifully prepared. Fish and chips, local pork ribs, seafood chowder (of course!), and other traditional dishes are served with flair and pride. The bar interior is beautifully designed and comfortable, taking patrons back to the heyday of the establishment's 1868 founding. An extensive wine

list, Irish whiskey shelf, and local craft brew selection combines with the fine food to create a perfect dining experience for all palates.

Afterward, take a stroll around town to walk off your lunch. A couple of blocks away, check out Dungarvan Castle, a strategic fortification built in the 12th century to guard the river and harbor here. (The prefix “Dun-“ means “fort”.)

If you head farther west on the N25 you’ll come to County Cork, and loop around to our first chapter. On the way you’ll pass **Ardmore**, a town famous for its hilltop 12th-century cathedral and round tower, both with many interesting features intact. This was the location of a 5th-century monastic settlement established by Saint Declan,

one of the oldest such sites—by most accounts, Declan predates Saint Patrick in Ireland by a few years. The coastal town itself is cute; stop in at the **Ardmore Gallery and Tea Room**, where you can get a coffee and a fresh scone, and check out the local art for sale hanging on the walls.

For now, head back east towards Waterford. This is one of the largest cities in Ireland, so unless you have a thing for fine crystal and heavy traffic, skirt the city to the south and follow the R683 to "Passage East". This is just what it sounds like—a car ferry ride across the River Barrow (which is really a bay at this point) between Counties Waterford and Wexford. The ride is inexpensive, quick (15 minutes or so), and picturesque, and it's the only way to cross the water for miles.

On the Wexford side the town is called Ballyhack. From here, find the R733 and head east, looking for signs to the south leading to **Tintern Abbey**. Legend has it that a famous and powerful 12th-century knight was caught in a violent storm at sea. He vowed to establish an abbey if he managed to land safely. He did so, and the result was this Cistercian abbey, founded in 1203. Monks from the Welsh abbey of the same name occupied it at first. After its dissolution in the 1500s, the property became the estate of the Colclough family, which restored some of the buildings for dwelling in the 16th century. The ruins are extensive, and the site includes woodland walking trails that explore the land around the abbey. Unlike many such abbey ruins, this one is a ticketed site, and includes a tea room and guided tours. Don't miss the 200-year-old Colcough walled gardens, on one of the forest paths.

From here, follow the little roads south. You'll be heading down the Hook Peninsula, a beautiful and largely undeveloped part of the county. The way is dotted with little historic sites, and a few big ones. One of the little ones that leaves a big impression is the **Templetown Church** ruins. On the road traversing the western length of the peninsula, this empty shell of a church and tower is what remains of a 12th-century settlement connected to the legendary Knights Templar. On an overcast and windy day, this bleak location and

the vine-covered stone walls create a ghostly atmosphere. A pint at the nearby Templar's Inn will take the edge off your fear of the spirits of Knights past... or will it? (Yes, it will.)

The terrain along the final stretch of road to the end of the narrowing peninsula becomes wilder. The coast is nearer, and more rocky. Signs warning of blowholes appear on little car pull-offs. Walk carefully here, if at all. Other signs warn not just of slippery rocks and unsafe currents but also of "freak waves". Soon, an obelisk appears, its black-and-white stripes stark against the sky. This is **Hook Point Lighthouse**, built in the 13th century to overlook Waterford Harbor and the Celtic Sea. It was an architectural marvel at the time, and today is the oldest working lighthouse in the world. A large visitor facility has been installed here, complete with a bookshop, a cafe, and an observatory, as well as the lighthouse and keepers' buildings. It is also a good spot for watching dolphins and whales. Ample parking invites tour buses, but at early hours or in the off-season this is a fascinating historical site and scenic destination.

Head back north now—maybe cross your fingers as you drive by the Templar's church—to **Duncannon**, not far south of the ferry at Ballyhack. This colorful little town is a microcosm of "Little Roads" interest, with good eating, interesting history, and unusual experiences. In this case, the latter involves driving on a one-kilometer strand of beach. Like the one in Rossnowlagh (see Itinerary 4), this beach is hard-packed sand, suitable for a drive out to the best tailgating spot ever. On a clear evening you can (theoretically) look from here across the Barrow estuary and see the light at Hook Peninsula. Above the beach are a series of homes, including the charming **Seashells**

B&B. The hosts here offer a nice full Irish breakfast—you'll smell it cooking when you awake—and their little breakfast room has a beautiful glass window view of the strand and the sea-scape beyond. At the end of the beach, **Duncannon Fortress** has perched atop these rocky cliffs since the 16th century. This is an imposing star-shaped fort with pointed bastions and round guard towers, a convincing protection of this vital water access to Waterford and the rest of southern Ireland.

Adjacent to the fort and the beach, the **Strand Tavern** offers the best food in the area—a traditional, fresh, and delicious experience in a charming old pub atmosphere. Burgers are made with quality Irish beef, and the traditional brown bread is warm right from the oven. Ask what's fresh and handmade that day, as well as what local craft brews are on tap. As this is a fishing village, their seafood chowder is a must. Even in a land of excellent chowders, this is one of the best.

An hour diversion east takes you towards Wexford. Turn south past Rosslare Harbor towards the southeastern tip of Ireland, and you'll reach the

remote food stop for which you've gone out of your way: **The Lobster Pot** in Carne. It's just what it sounds like, and the seafood here is as fresh as it comes. Nearby is a historical and picturesque curiosity, unique in Ireland—the oldest intact windmill in the country. The thatch-roofed **Tacumshane Windmill** was built in the 1840s. Its inner workings were originally built from wood salvaged from nearby shipwrecks. (Don't worry—the lobster fishermen's boats are perfectly safe these days, and therefore so are your lunch prospects.) The offerings of this little corner of Ireland are emblematic of our Little Roads philosophy: Landscapes only seldom trod, evocative places, and delicious local food prepared by those who know it best.

Restaurants are open every day for lunch and dinner unless otherwise noted.

Wicklow

Phil Healy's Pub

Family-run pub in Wicklow town with a large menu, beautiful interior space, and good craft beers on tap. Great "pub grub".

https://www.facebook.com/philhealys/

Duncannon

The Strand Tavern Seafood Bar

Family-run pub specializing in seafood. Many menu items sourced from local vendors. An interesting note: the bar counter and shelves are made from wood reclaimed from the Alfred D. Snow, which wrecked and washed ashore in 1888.

http://www.strandtavern.ie/

Dungarvan

Merry's Bar and Restaurant

Absolutely gorgeous bar, worth a visit just to see the interior, but gratefully the food is stunning as well. Everything handmade and locally sourced. Don't miss dessert.

https://www.facebook.com/merrysgastropub/?rf=356251747774020

Kilkenny

Hibernian Hotel Bar

Another one of those pubs that is too beautiful to believe, in winter ask for a table by the open bar. Top notch food and service.

http://www.kilkennyhibernianhotel.com/

Left Bank and Rive Gauche

Award-winning gastropub in the heart of Kilkenny. Left Bank serves pub grub, Rive Gauche serves French-inspired dinners. They are in the same historic bank building, now a stylish, modern bar and restaurant.

https://www.leftbank.ie/

Marble City Bar

Upstairs is a gastropub, downstairs a tearoom. One of the oldest public houses in the county, the owners have remodeled it with modern, contemporary flair. Excellent traditional pub grub. Owned by the same folks who own Langton's.

http://www.langtons.ie/bars/marble-city-bar/

Carne

The Lobster Pot

Absolutely adorable pub specializing in seafood at the very tip of the southeast corner of Ireland. Excellent fresh seafood, if you order a lobster here you'll choose your own. Staff told us they stopped naming them, saying it was hard to say "Well, there goes Fred".

Open Wednesday - Sunday for lunch and dinner. Reservations recommended.

http://lobsterpotwexford.com/

Wicklow

Wicklow Head Lighthouse

We adore this lighthouse, which is the only one we know where you rent the actual lighthouse, and not the lighthouse keeper's cabins. There are two bedrooms, a cozy sitting room near the top, and the kitchen at the top level 109 steps up!

Remote, gorgeous, serene. Be sure to ask the host which way to park your car so the winds whipping off the cliffs don't rip your car door off.

2 night stay minimum, from 550€ per 2 night stay
http://www.irishlandmark.com/

Kilkenny

Langton House Hotel

This boutique hotel looks small from the street but inside is a maze of gorgeous, huge ballrooms and dining rooms. They light real candles at night in some of the hallways. Rooms are upstairs, downstairs you'll find a restaurant and a couple of bars, including our favorite, Bridie's. Extremely affordable considering everything you are getting. Full Irish breakfast cooked to order in the morning, also several other breakfast options.

Doubles from 80€.
http://www.langtons.ie/

Duncannon

Seashells B&B

We booked Seashells for the views of Waterford Harbor, and we were not disappointed. The common room has stunning views, you can sit at the table, pour yourself a glass of wine and watch the waves. We prefer the "Double Beach Room", which is right next to the common room, and has huge picture windows looking out on the sea. Full Irish breakfast cooked to order in the morning by the affable hosts.

Doubles from 80€.

http://seashells.ie/

Sights are free to enter unless otherwise noted.

Glendalough, Black Castle, Castleruddery stone circle, Brownshill portal tomb, Timahoe church and round tower, Kilcooley Abbey, Kells Priory, Duiske Abbey, Kilree monastic site, Kilkieran cemetery, Ardmore round tower, Tintern Abbey, Templetown church, Hook Point Lighthouse, Tacumshane Windmill.

Kilmacthomas

Mayfield Birds of Prey

Anyone mildly interested in birds of prey will want to book here. You will have the chance to hold, feed, and fly multiple birds, including owls, falcons, and hawks. If the weather is sunny, you will be outdoors; if it's rainy, you still get to fly them in a large warehouse. A unique experience. Their handler Willie tells you all about them, their habits and history, and his rapport with the birds is obvious and endearing.

Children's rate from 6€, adults from 15€, family bookings also available.

http://falconryinireland.com/

Hook Peninsula

Hook Peninsula Lighthouse

The oldest lighthouse in the world, at the tip of the beautiful Hook Peninsula. Guided tours are available, which allow you to climb the tower and take in the views from the balcony. There is a cafe and bakery on site as well.

Open every day 9:30 - 6, cafe closes at 5:30.

http://www.hookheritage.ie/

Tinahely

Tinahely Farm Shop and Cafe

A very well-stocked farm shop with local meats, cheeses, produce, and loads of Irish products that will be very appealing to foodies. There is a lovely little cafe here where you can have a special lunch. There is also an activity barn for the kids, so you can come here and make a day of it. The cafe serves espresso and cappuccino.

Open Tuesday - Saturday 9:30 - 5, Sunday 10:30 - 5. Closed Mondays.

http://tinahelyfarm.ie/

Avoca

Avoca Handweavers

The oldest working wool mill in Ireland. You can watch the wool being woven in the shop, and have lunch at the cafe here. Upstairs there is a selection of items on sale or clearance for those looking for a bargain. Open every day.

Shop hours: Winter 9:30 - 5, Summer 9:30 - 6. Mill closes at 4:30. Cafe open 9:30 - 5.

http://www.avocahandweavers.com/

Castelcomer

Susan Boland Pottery

Susan's ceramic shop is one of several artist's shops located in the Castlecomer Discovery Park, a little haven of artisans well worth visiting. Her kiln is right in the shop, and it's interesting to see her works in process as her shop is also her studio. This is a perfect place to stop and buy yourself a huge, sea-blue handmade ceramic mug for your morning tea or coffee.

Closed Mondays, but since this is Susan's shop, her hours may be flexible.

https://susanbolandceramics.com/

Thomastown

The Truffle Fairy

Award-winning chocalatier in the little artsy town of Thomastown. Many of the truffle varieties inspired by alcohol, such as tequila/lime/salt or vodka/raspberry. In addition to truffles, you can also find fudge, chocolate bars, and good coffee here.

Open Monday - Saturday 10 - 5.

http://trufflefairy.ie/

Graiguenamanagh

Cushendale Woolen Mills

Family-run woolen mill. If you want locally-sourced wool, and you want to meet the producers, this is the place for you. This is a tiny shop, and is has the good fortune of being located in a small town with plenty of unique things to see.

Open Monday - Friday 8:30 - 5:30 (closed 12:30 - 1:30); Saturday 10 - 1

http://cushendale.ie/

ROUTE #8

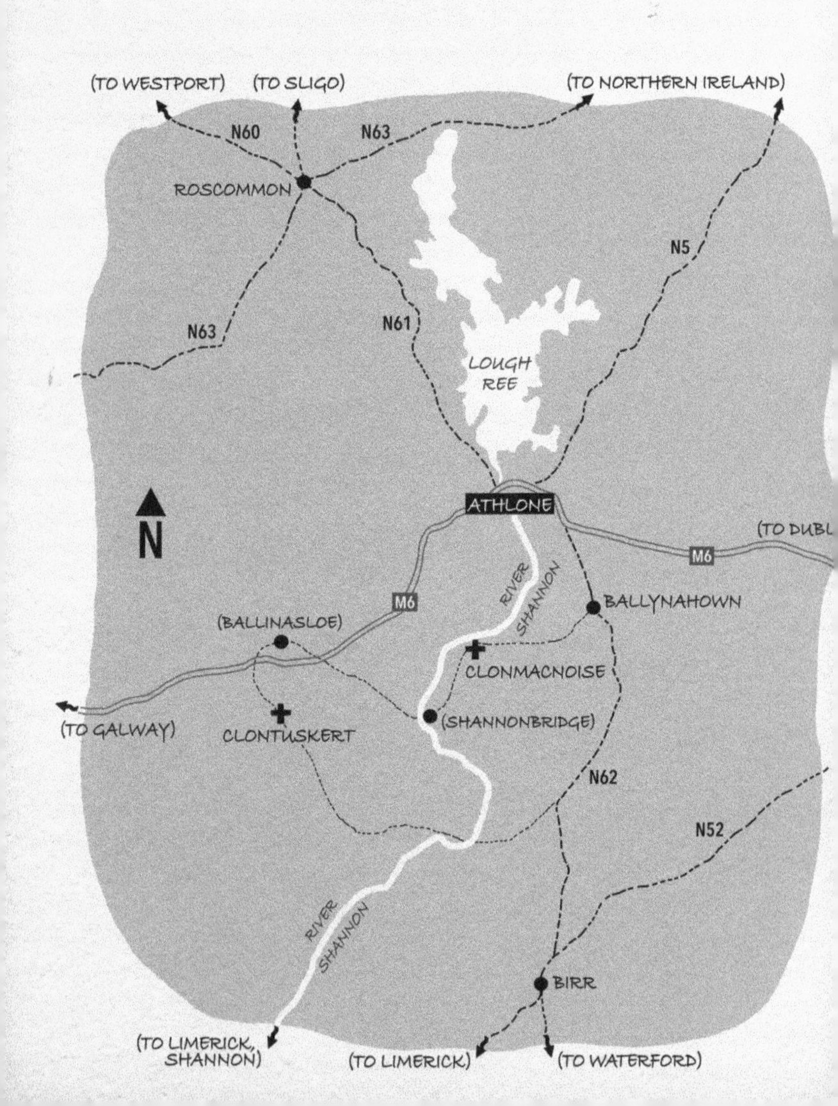

(TO WESTPORT)
(TO SLIGO)
(TO NORTHERN IRELAND)
N60
N63
ROSCOMMON
N5
N61
N63
LOUGH REE
ATHLONE
N
(TO DUBL
M6
RIVER SHANNON
M6
BALLYNAHOWN
(BALLINASLOE)
CLONMACNOISE
(SHANNONBRIDGE)
(TO GALWAY)
CLONTUSKERT
N62
N52
RIVER SHANNON
BIRR
(TO LIMERICK, SHANNON)
(TO LIMERICK)
(TO WATERFORD)

Central Ireland

When we travel in Ireland, we personally find ourselves drawn to the coastal areas, so we don't always delve deeply into the central Irish counties, a.k.a. The Midlands. Nevertheless, over the years we've found a handful of places of great interest between our various Points A and B. And of course there are countless more still to be discovered. It's worth remembering that any given point in Ireland is, at most, only a couple of hours drive from the coast, so the destinations in this itinerary can easily be connected to one or more of our previous itineraries.

At the geographical center of Ireland is the town of **Athlone** (County Westmeath) on the River Shannon at the south end of Lough Ree. The M4/M6 east-west highway from Dublin to Galway passes right through town. Its strategic position—the river crossing here is the only one for 40 kilometers in either direction—made the town a hub for trade and culture for centuries. It's a bustling town with a rich heritage. The 12th-century castle at the center of town is now an interactive museum detailing the history of Athlone and the Midlands. Around the corner from the castle is the historic Sean's Bar, famous for its claim to be the oldest bar in Ireland, a claim the Guinness Book of World Records supports. Archaeologists at this location discovered remains of wall structures dating from the 10th century. A bit of this wall is on display in the bar, as well as coins from the same era that were evidently minted by innkeepers as a means of settling bar tabs. Today the pub serves food as well as its own brews, including their tasty "900 AD" lager.

Ireland's inland waterways

Visitors to the Midlands, particularly to the river town of Athlone may be surprised to see some large boats in the local lakes and rivers In fact, the River Shannon extends from Limerick in the west up through these Midland counties. Boats can traverse the waters from the Shannon Estuary north through a series of locks and dams all the way to the lake at Athlone and beyond, almost as far north as Sligo. Moreover, from the northernmost point of the Shannon, boats can cross through the Shannon-Erne Waterway to the lakes of Lough Erne (Itinerary 5) in Northern Ireland, and so out to the sea again near Donegal Harbor (Itinerary 4). Serious boaters might well decide to experience Ireland in a new way—exploring the Little Loughs rather than the Little Roads...

A few blocks from the castle is the **Prince of Wales Hotel**, a facility with an attached nightclub, pub, and restaurant. Next to this hotel is the early 19th-century Saint Mary's Church and its little graveyard, which seems incongruous in the midst of this modern commercial district. Next to the church is a huge shopping center, attached to which is another in

congruity: **The Fatted Calf**, an award-winning restaurant focusing on using locally sourced ingredients to create modern international plates. For example, their pork belly dish uses meat from Horan's butchers, whose storefront you'll see from your table in the restaurant. Though this is not traditional Irish cuisine, it is local eating at its best.

From Athlone's west bank, the N61 road goes up the west side of Lough Ree to the county town of **Roscommon**. (Note that we touched upon this county from the west, when venturing to the abbey ruin at Frenchpark in Itinerary 3.) In the center of Roscommon, you'll see the storefront of **Castlemine Farm Shop**. Castlemine, an old family-run livestock farm, offers high-quality lamb, beef, and pork cuts from their well-tended animals. Stock up here on house-made sausages, meat and vegetable pies, or basic butcher products—this is the best there is. Tours of their countryside farm can be arranged with advance notice.

On the north edge of town—look for Castle Street—you'll find a 14-acre county park, on which sits the remains of **Roscommon Castle**. The fortification was built in the 13th century. Like many such strongholds, it changed hands many times in subsequent eras, so it contains centuries of stonework and history. The park includes walking and jogging paths and a duck pond. It's amazing that the locals get to exercise right next to an 800-year-old monument.

Northeast of Athlone, the back roads beyond Mullingar contain a couple of oddities worth mentioning. In the vicinity of Clonkill, you may pass by a house with a couple of odd domes in the yard. Resident John Nooney has turned his little rural house into the **Clonkill**

Observatory, an amateur but dedicated astronomy center, with museum-style exhibits about space exploration and two domed observatories visible from the road. The night sky in this remote and sparsely populated countryside must be stunning with stars, making this a sensible location for a stargazing endeavor. (Note that this is County Westmeath; you're a mere half-hour from the cairns at Loughcrew, County Meath, in Itinerary 6, another easy connection between this itinerary and those previous.) A few more turns take you to the crossroads at Crookedwood. Go east from Murray's pub and look for brown signs to the old **Taghmon Church** (a.k.a. St Munna's Church), built in the 15th century on the site of a monastery founded a thousand years earlier by Saint Munna (a.k.a. Saint Fintan—the early Christians sometimes had trouble keeping names straight). This one has defensive features normally found on castles or strategic guard towers rather than on churches: It has a crenellated, 4-story tower house with "machicolations", protruding portals through which defenders could pour hot oil or drop projectiles on potential attackers. A few interesting carved figures adorn the church, including a warding "Sheela-na-gig". This is a grotesque female figure that can be found on some churches of this era, likely coming from an earlier structure and harkening back to pagan traditions.

South of Lough Ree and Athlone, the N62 leads to a little crossroads and the even littler village of **Ballynahown**. Look for the small church/town hall in the center of town. Next to it is a "rockery", a pebble garden with a miniature rock representation of a nearby medieval monastery. (More on this in a bit.) Ballynahown is a haven of sorts for artists, and features several craft studios and shops. The **Celtic Roots Studio**, next door to the town hall, specializes in sculpture and jewelry made from aged bog wood, the remains of trees submerged for centuries in the Midlands' peat bogs. The shop is also part of the worldwide "Économusée" network of artisan museums that highlight important aspects of cultural traditions.

From the crossroads, take the little road running southwest. It meets the R444 and continues west to the ancient grounds of **Clonmacnoise**. This is the monastery represented by Ballynahown's rockery—an extensive monastic acreage right on the Shannon River. Saint Ciaran the Younger founded Clonmacnoise in 538 AD. Because he was buried here, the place became—and still is—a heavily visited pilgrimage destination. Legend has it that Ciaran, like Jesus, was the son of a carpenter who died at age 33. Unlike Jesus, he had a prodigious cow who could provide milk for the whole monastery. (This last story may have been borrowed from the Saint Kevin legend, or vice-versa—see Itinerary 6.)

Stroll in the shadow of the looming 12th-century round tower. Explore the remains of the temples and cathedral dating from as early as the 10th century. Examine the Biblical scenes carved on the three Celtic High Crosses—and these are *really* high. The walled grounds are accessible only through the visitor's center/museum, where you can see the real crosses (those in the yard are replicas) now kept inside the museum to preserve them from the sands of time.

This is another place that despite its remoteness can be crowded in high season, so plan accordingly. Visit early in the day, or in the off-season. Nearby the monastic settlement stand the weirdly askew ruins of a Norman castle, built in the 13th century as a military outpost to guard the river route. Erosion and geological upheaval have rendered the castle unstable, so don't approach it, as you can never know if today might be the day it decides to finally topple over the cliffs into the river below.

The R444 highway follows the river south to Shannonbridge, where you can, naturally, cross the bridge over the River Shannon. From there, the R357 goes northwest to Ballinasloe, which is the only place for a long way to cross the tributary River Suck. All this is to get over to the R355 which leads south and east again. Why did you just drive all this way, and so circuitously? One reason is that the rivers in this particular area make things complicated. The other is that you'll want to see this next place, one of the loneliest places we've found.

About six kilometers south of Ballinasloe, the ruins of **Clontuskert Abbey** are visible from the road in the middle of nowhere, surrounded by farmlands and pastures. Built on the remains of an 8th-century abbey, this Augustinian priory was

built in the 13th century, burned in the 14th and rebuilt in the 15th, only to be "suppressed" by Henry VIII in the 16th. The site is small but full of interesting stonework and carvings in its archways, windows, and gravestones. A row of columns in the cloisters outlines a long hall ending in what must have been the kitchen oven. As of this writing, a long-neglected statue of Jesus leans against the outer wall at the rear of the grounds. Only the cows keep him company now. A small stone-walled lot offers parking next to an old metal farm shed right at the highway; or you can drive down the little farm road (a few hundred meters) right up to the abbey, where there's room for a couple of cars—probably one more space than is needed for this remote and deserted place. (As remote as it is here, you're now a scant hour's drive from Moran's Oyster Cottage south of Galway in Itinerary 2.)

If you don't want to cross to the west side of the Shannon just yet, you can continue south from

Ballynahown on the N62. After about 30 kilometers you'll come to **Birr**, another crossroads town but much smaller than Athlone. (From Birr it is about an hour drive southeast to the abbey at Kilcooley or the round tower at Timahoe, described in Itinerary 7.)

Birr's **Emmett House B&B** offers travelers a quaint and cute place to stay—an 18th-century guest house right on the center town square. Across the square is the 18th-century hotel and restaurant, **Dooly's**. Their pub/restaurant is nice and simple, with a good draft selection—several

local craft brews are prominent. There is also an attached coffee shop where they bake their own scones. Our favorite eatery in town is a couple of blocks south of the square: **Bramble's Café and Delicatessen**, which makes all its food with local, organic ingredients—vegetables and fruit, eggs, cheeses, meats—and strives for a "green" footprint at all times. Their quiches, sausage pies, and soups are favorites among the locals, so the lines may be lengthy, but the food is definitely worth waiting for. (This, by the way, is an important hallmark of the way we like to travel: For the best eating, find out where the locals like to go.)

A couple of blocks away stands a 17th-century castle house (built on medieval ruins) that is now home to **Birr Castle**, its beautiful gardens, and the **Birr Science Center**. Here, in 1845, the Irish astronomer William Parsons built a 52-foot long telescope, the largest in the world for 70 years. With it, he made several vital astronomical discoveries, including the spiral nature of galaxies. As a result, Birr became a center of engineering, astronomy, and photography in the 19th and 20th centuries. Visitors can explore the castle museum, wander the gardens, and see the huge telescope, which is still working today.

The Midlands of Ireland are rich with fascinating places to visit, landscapes to take in, and delicious things to eat—and drink! The destinations in this itinerary are just a few of the things we've found over the years, just as all the places in this book are but a sampling of the wonderful things you can find if you're willing to forego the familiar for a drive down the little roads.

Birr

Brambles Cafe and Deli

A delightful surprise tucked down a small side street. The cafe uses locally sourced, organic food. Large variety of bakery items baked in-house, including several types of bread. This is where you want to come to have a healthy, hearty breakfast or lunch, or to stop and treat yourself to a cappuccino and slice of cake. You can also buy locally made jams, loaves of bread, local produce, and fresh duck or hen eggs here.

Open Monday - Saturday 8:30 - 6, Sunday 11 - 2:30.
http://www.bramblesbirr.ie/

Athlone

The Fatted Calf

Award-winning gastropub in the center of Athlone. Modern, contemporary decor with a friendly staff. The kitchen is within view of the tables so you can get a sneak peek of your dinner being prepared. Lots of locally sourced ingredients paired with international flavors; great attention to presentation as well as flavor.

Open for dinner Tuesday - Saturday. Open for lunch Thursday - Saturday. Closed Sunday and Monday. Reservations recommended.

http://www.thefattedcalf.ie

Athlone

Sean's Bar

We did not eat here, and honestly we don't even know if they have food. But we are listing this because it is the oldest pub in the world, according to the Guinness Book of Records. The pub was opened in 900AD. Stop by and have a pint of their own brew (called "900AD", of course), and check out the thousands of mementos plastered on the walls.

http://www.seansbar.ie/home

Birr

Emmett House B&B

Located right on Birr's Emmet Square, Emmett House dates to the early 1700's and many of the rooms have four-poster beds. Full Irish breakfast served in the dining room.

Doubles from 75€.

http://www.emmethouse.com/

Athlone

Prince of Wales Hotel

Comfortable, boutique hotel on Athlone's main square. You can park your car in their (free) lot, and spend the day walking around this (for us) fairly large town. From here to Dublin Airport is only 1.5 hours. Directly across the street from this hotel is the excellent gastropub The Fatted Calf.

Doubles from 60€.

http://www.theprinceofwales.ie/

Sights are free to enter unless otherwise noted.

Clontuskert Abbey, Roscommon Castle, Taghmon church, Clonkill Observatory.

Athlone

Athlone Castle

This castle is in the center of the town on the river, across from the cathedral. This is a family-friendly attraction with lots of activities for children and grown-ups kids alike. Open daily, 10 - 6; hours are shorter in winter months. Admission: Adults 8€, reductions for children/seniors.

www.athlonecastle.ie

Birr

Birr Castle, Gardens, and Science Center

This 17th-century castle is on a walled estate with beautiful gardens and an important astronomy center featuring a 52-foot telescope from the 1800s. Open daily, 9 - 6; hours are shorter in winter months. Admission: Adults 9€, reductions for children/students/seniors/families.

http://birrcastle.com/

Ballynahown

Clonmacnoise

Hours vary seasonally, but in general open 10 - 6. Last admission 45 minutes before closing.

Admission 8€ for adults, reduced rates for seniors and students.

http://www.heritageireland.ie/en/midlands-east-coast/clonmacnoise/

Roscommon

Castlemine Farm Shop

This is a fairly small farm shop, which specializes in meats (raised on their farm, of course). You can find some produce and cheese here, but we recommend coming here just to pick up a couple of their ready-made pies (savory, not sweet).

http://castleminefarm.ie/retail-store/

APPENDIX 1

Passports

Your US passport must be valid for six months after the last date of your trip. If your passport expires in October and your trip ends in May, you will not be able to board the plane.

If you need a new passport or need to renew your old one, the State Department recommends doing that at least 6 weeks in advance. We recommend 3 months, just to avoid the stress of frantically checking the mail every day. We also highly recommend applying for Global Entry, which will greatly expedite your time waiting in line at both ends of your trip.

Driving in Ireland

For those cultures that drive on the "right" (no pun intended), the number one challenge of driving in Ireland is driving on the left side of the road. It may be worth the extra money to secure a rental that has automatic transmission, enabling the driver to devote more brain-power to driving on the left side of the road from the right side of the car.

So, for right turns, you must yield to the oncoming traffic (rather than for left turns as elsewhere). It's the left turns, then, are the easier ones to make. Note, however, that there is no equivalent of "right on red" in Ireland (it would be left on red there). A red light is a red light, period.

In the Irish Road System, the equivalent of the multi-lane, limited-access Interstate (U.S.) or Autostrada/Autobahn (continental Europe) highway is the Motorway, marked M1, M50, and so on. There are only a few stretches of this kind of highway in the country. The big network of highways is the National Road system (marked N60, N71, etc). These highways can be multi-lane divided highways, but just as often they're simple two-lane roads. Smaller regional or local roads, if they're numbered at all, are marked with R or L before the route number. These can be narrow, sometimes just one lane for both directions. In this case, oncoming drivers must cooperate to pass one another at the occasional driveway or wide spot in the road. (In Northern Ireland as in the rest of the U.K. the roads are designated "A" and "B" rather than "N" and "R".)

Roundabouts

As in other parts of Europe, roundabouts or traffic circles are common in place of large stop-light intersections. Remember that the traffic flows from right to left, or clockwise. Approach the circle, look right and bear left, yielding to cars already in the circle. Look for the signs directing you to your next destination, and you can signal your exit (to the left!) from the circle. Don't be afraid (or embarrassed) to go around the circle an extra time or three, if you're uncertain which road to take from the circle. The only people who will notice your extra revolutions are doing it themselves.

Speed limits

Rules of the road are taken seriously in Ireland. Speed limits are no exception, so observe postings carefully. One good sign to know is the round white sign with a black slash, indicating the "National Speed Limit". This is 120 kph for Motorways, 100 for the National "N" roads, and 80 for "R" or "L" roads. Watch for reduced speed limit areas, especially when approaching towns, school zones, and crosswalks.

Make driving safety your number one priority. Be prepared to miss your turn, or miss your exit on the highway, or pull over, rather than risk an accident while making a last minute correction. Always build extra time into your daily travel plans for turning around, getting lost, or, if you're lucky, unexpectedly finding an interesting new place to visit.

Money

Nearly all restaurants and hotels accept credit cards, but a few still do not, so make sure you know before you buy. Certainly use cash in a pub if you're buying a single pint, or at a café for a tea/coffee. Bars will usually accept cards, but out of courtesy, use cash unless the tab is at least into double-digits.

Note: We've found that many places that do accept cards do not accept American Express, since their commission fees are so high. Mastercard and VISA are generally fine.

Check with your bank about international ATM withdrawal fees. We use ATMs there as needed, as the exchange rate is the same or close to what you will find at the airport. (Traveler's checks have gone the way of wooden dentures, so don't even ask.)

Exchange counters at the airport often offer "deals" that allow you to exchange unspent currency on your trip back without fees. Alternatively, you can just keep track of your spending in general and work your way down to zero Euros/Pounds at the end of your trip.

As of this writing, most American credit cards are embedded with a chip, but using one in Ireland still requires a signature. When you insert your card into a machine, the clerk/ bartender will usually hand the device to you, expecting you to enter your PIN. Tell them that it's a U.S. card that will want your signature; they know how to deal with that and you'll be paid up and on your way in no time.

Wi-Fi / cellular data

Free Wi-Fi is available at many B&Bs, restaurants and bars. You can call your phone company and have an international data package added for a month. That said, we recommend just using the Wi-Fi when you find it. Better yet, take a break from constantly being tethered to your phone. You'll be amazed at how much more you experience things around you when you are not focused on staring at a small screen.

Packing

It's impossible to overstate the importance of packing light for a good trip, for two reasons: 1) You want the most mobility and flexibility, so your focus is on experiencing the place you are visiting rather than managing the mound of stuff in your suitcase; and 2) the goal is to arrive with very little, and leave with bags laden down with all the goodies you'll find. Trust us, you'll be disappointed if you can't buy that bottle of craft ale or jar of z jam because you had to make room for your hairdryer/extra shoes/umbrella. We've traveled overseas dozens of times, and we offer extensive advice on packing smart on our website, http://www.LittleRoadsEurope.com.

A planning note

Many of the small places we list in this book are, to our knowledge, not listed anywhere else. We have made every effort to accumulate and update the information in this book; however, small businesses can shut down or be closed unexpectedly for illnesses, vacations, or just because they felt like it. Many of the places we list have websites and/or Facebook pages; we suggest you confirm their opening days/times before visiting to avoid disappointment. Without limit, we are not responsible for any distress, disappointment, or damage incurred by following this guide. However, if you do find information that you think could use updating, please let us know by contacting us via email at littleroadseurope@gmail.com.

http://www.LittleRoadsEurope.com

Thank you!

We hope you've enjoyed this book. For more information on the places we travel, please visit us at www.LittleRoadsEurope.com.

Interested in other parts of Europe? Check out our award-winning guidebooks to Italy: **Emilia-Romagna: A Personal Guide to Little-known Places Foodies Will Love** and **Tuscany: Small-town Itineraries for the Foodie Traveler**. Find out how we apply our travel philosophy to exploring these beautiful regions of Italy, visiting its historic small towns, and of course eating its famously fantastic food.

If you're thinking about a trip to Ireland or Italy, we hope you'll consider our Itinerary Building Service. We design custom itineraries for clients based on our extensive travel experiences in Ireland and the northern regions of Italy. Working from your preferences, we'll help you navigate these regions, make reservations, visit artisans, and give recommendations for a trip that is authentic, immersive, memorable and affordable. Start your vacation before you even leave, and let us do the hard part!

- Zeneba & Matt

Little Roads Europe Travel Guide Series

ACKNOWLEDGEMENTS

Thanks to:

Kristin Whittlesey, for her unwavering encouragement and her indispensible editing;

Robert Firpo-Cappiello of Budget Travel and Nancy Cleary of Wyatt-MacKenzie, for their support and advice;

Tony Macaulay and Leslie Dixon for their kind words and support;

Laura Atkinson, for her continued creativity and map designs;

our visionary friends Sandy Obodzinski and Laura Alabed-Olsson, who first gave us the idea to create Little Roads Europe;

and Andi Bordick, whose essential knowledge, skills, and efforts made it possible to develop our website, our brand, and our business.

Thanks also to the countless chefs, innkeepers, artisans, and guides we've listed in this book, who have inspired us over the years to develop our Little Roads travel philosophy.

Notes

Notes

CPSIA information can be obtained
at www.ICGtesting.com
Printed in the USA
LVHW06s1040230518
578163LV00007B/38/P